First World War
and Army of Occupation
War Diary
France, Belgium and Germany

15 DIVISION
46 Infantry Brigade,
Brigade Machine Gun Company
7 February 1916 - 28 February 1918

WO95/1954/3

The Naval & Military Press Ltd
www.nmarchive.com
Published in association with The National Archives

Published by

The Naval & Military Press Ltd

Unit 10 Ridgewood Industrial Park,

Uckfield, East Sussex,

TN22 5QE England

Tel: +44 (0) 1825 749494

www.naval-military-press.com

www.nmarchive.com

This diary has been reprinted in facsimile from the original. Any imperfections are inevitably reproduced and the quality may fall short of modern type and cartographic standards.

© **Crown Copyright**
Images reproduced by permission of The National Archives, London, England, 2015.

Contents

Document type	Place/Title	Date From	Date To
Heading	WO95/1954/3		
Heading	15th Division. 46th Infy Bde. 46th Machine Gun Coy. Feb 1916-Feb 1918		
Heading	15th 46th Bde. M.G. Coy. Vol. I.		
Heading	Diary of No. 46 Brigade Machine Gun Company (Feb 7th-Feb 29th).		
War Diary	Grantham.	07/02/1916	08/02/1916
War Diary	Southampton.	08/02/1916	08/02/1916
War Diary	Havre.	09/02/1916	12/02/1916
War Diary	Noeux-Les-Mines.	12/02/1916	12/02/1916
War Diary	Mazingabe	13/02/1916	25/02/1916
War Diary	Gosnay.	26/02/1916	29/02/1916
Heading	War Diary of No. 46 Brigade Machine Gun Company March 1st-March 31st. 46 M B Coy. Vol. 2		
War Diary	Mazingarbe.	01/03/1916	14/03/1916
War Diary	Gosnay.	15/03/1916	19/03/1916
War Diary	Mazingarbe.	19/03/1916	25/03/1916
War Diary	Noeux-Les-Mines.	26/03/1916	26/03/1916
War Diary	Gosnay.	27/03/1916	31/03/1916
Heading	Diary of No. 46 Bgde M.G. Coy. April 1st-30th. Vol. 3		
War Diary	Gosnay.	01/04/1916	01/04/1916
War Diary	Mazingarbe.	01/04/1916	11/04/1916
War Diary	Raimbert.	12/04/1916	23/04/1916
War Diary	Vermelles.	24/04/1916	30/04/1916
Heading	War Diary of 46th Brigade Machine Gun Company (May 1st-May 31st). 46 M.G. Coy. Vol. 4		
War Diary	Trenches.	01/05/1916	01/05/1916
War Diary	Bethune.	02/05/1916	10/05/1916
War Diary	Noyelles.	11/05/1916	26/05/1916
War Diary	Bethune.	27/05/1916	27/05/1916
War Diary	Noyelles.	28/05/1916	31/05/1916
Heading	War Diary of 46th Brigade Machine Gun Company (June 1st-June 30th). 46 M.G. Coy. Vol. 5		
War Diary	Noyelles.	01/06/1916	30/06/1916
Heading	War Diary 46 M.G. Coy. from 1st July to 31st July 1916. Vol. 6		
Heading	War Diary 46th Brigade M.G. Coy. (July 1st-July 31st).		
War Diary	Noyelles.	01/07/1916	13/07/1916
War Diary	Bethune.	14/07/1916	21/07/1916
War Diary	Marles Les Mines.	22/07/1916	22/07/1916
War Diary	Heuchin.	23/07/1916	26/07/1916
War Diary	Blangermont	27/07/1916	27/07/1916
War Diary	Wavans	28/07/1916	29/07/1916
War Diary	Berneuil	30/07/1916	31/07/1916
Heading	46th Brigade. 15th Division. 46th Brigade Machine Gun Company August 1916		
Heading	War Diary of 46th Machine Gun Company (august 1st-august 31st). 46 M.G.E. Vol. 7		
War Diary	Flesselles.	01/08/1916	04/08/1916
War Diary	Flesselles Molliens au Bois.	04/08/1916	05/08/1916

War Diary	Franvillers	06/08/1916	06/08/1916
War Diary	Fricourt.	07/08/1916	19/08/1916
War Diary	Albert.	20/08/1916	27/08/1916
War Diary	Mametze	28/08/1916	31/08/1916
Heading	War Diary 46th Machine Gun Company (Sept 1st-Sept 30th). Vol. 8		
War Diary	Mametz Wood.	01/09/1916	03/09/1916
War Diary	Mametz.	03/09/1916	05/09/1916
War Diary	Fricourt.	06/09/1916	12/09/1916
War Diary	Contalmaison.	13/09/1916	18/09/1916
War Diary	Lavieville	19/09/1916	19/09/1916
War Diary	Lahoussoye	20/09/1916	30/09/1916
Miscellaneous	Report G V T.H.L. Farm 46 M.G.C.		
Miscellaneous	M.G. Report 15/17/9/16		
Miscellaneous	Report on action of M.G's 46 Coy during attach on 15th ink.		
Miscellaneous			
Miscellaneous	A Form. Messages And Signals.		
Miscellaneous	Action of 46th Trench Mortar Battery, 46th Brigade during advance on 15th, 16th and 17th September 1916	20/09/1916	20/09/1916
Heading	War Diary October 1916. M.G. Coy. Vol. 9		
War Diary	Albert.	01/10/1916	09/10/1916
War Diary	Fricourt.	10/10/1916	14/10/1916
War Diary	Martinpuich.	15/10/1916	19/10/1916
War Diary	Fricourt.	20/10/1916	31/10/1916
Heading	War Diary. 46 Machine Gun Coy. from 1/11/16 to 30/11/16		
War Diary	Lonely Trench.	01/11/1916	01/11/1916
War Diary	Millencourt.	02/11/1916	05/11/1916
War Diary	Henencourt Wood.	06/11/1916	15/11/1916
War Diary	Naours.	16/11/1916	27/11/1916
War Diary	Warloy.	28/11/1916	30/11/1916
Heading	H.Q. 15th Divn. Herewith War Diary for December. 46 M.G. Coy. Vol. XI.		
War Diary	Warloy.	01/12/1916	02/12/1916
War Diary	Becourt Wood.	03/12/1916	23/12/1916
War Diary	Shelter Wood Camp.	24/12/1916	31/12/1916
Heading	H.Q. 15th Divn. Herewith please find War Diary for Jan 1917. 46 M G Coy. Vol. 12		
War Diary		01/01/1917	31/01/1917
Miscellaneous	Headquarters 15th Divn. Herewith Please find War Diary for Feb 1917 46 M.G. Coy Vol 13		
War Diary	Albert	01/02/1917	04/02/1917
War Diary	Warloy	05/02/1917	13/02/1917
War Diary	Beauval	14/02/1917	14/02/1917
War Diary	Gezaincourt.	15/02/1917	15/02/1917
War Diary	Bonnieres	16/02/1917	16/02/1917
War Diary	Villers Sir-Simon	17/02/1917	22/02/1917
War Diary	Arras	23/02/1917	28/02/1917
Heading	H.Q. 15th Divn. 46 M.G. Coy Vol 14		
War Diary	Arras	01/03/1917	02/03/1917
War Diary	Noyellette	03/03/1917	10/03/1917
War Diary	Gouy-En-Ternois	11/03/1917	18/03/1917
War Diary	Arras	19/03/1917	31/03/1917
War Diary	Arras	24/03/1917	31/03/1917
Heading	H.Q. 15th Divn. Herewith War Diary for April 1917		

War Diary	Arras	01/04/1917	01/04/1917
War Diary	Duisans	01/04/1917	05/04/1917
War Diary	Arras	06/04/1917	09/04/1917
War Diary	Operations.		
War Diary	Arras	12/04/1917	14/04/1917
War Diary	Duisans	15/04/1917	21/04/1917
War Diary	Operations		
War Diary		26/04/1917	30/04/1917
Map	Map A		
Map	Map B		
Miscellaneous	Report No.		
Map	Map C		
Miscellaneous	Sent At 0.15. p.m.		
Heading	War Diary Of 46th M.G. Company From 1st May 1917 To 31st May 1917 Vol 16		
War Diary	Duisans	01/05/1917	07/05/1917
War Diary	Fosseux	08/05/1917	21/05/1917
War Diary	Beaudricourt	22/05/1917	22/05/1917
War Diary	Bonnieres	23/05/1917	23/05/1917
War Diary	Haravesnes	24/05/1917	31/05/1917
Heading	War Diary Of 46th Machine Gun Company From 1-6-17 To 30-6-17. Vol 17		
Heading	H.Q. 46th L.B. Herewith War Diary for June 1917		
War Diary	Haravesnes	01/06/1917	30/06/1917
Heading	War Diary 46th Machine Gun Coy July 1917 Vol 18		
Miscellaneous	H.Q. 46th L.B.	06/08/1917	06/08/1917
War Diary	Brandhoek	01/07/1917	01/07/1917
War Diary	Watou	02/07/1917	08/07/1917
War Diary	Buysscheure	09/07/1917	30/07/1917
Miscellaneous	Narrative Of Operation Commanding On 31/7/17	31/07/1917	31/07/1917
Miscellaneous	H.Q. 46th L.B.	05/09/1917	05/09/1917
Heading	War Diary Of 46th Machine Gun Company From 1st August 1917 To 31st August 1917 Vol 19 15 Divn.		
War Diary		01/08/1917	16/08/1917
Miscellaneous	Narrative Of Operations From 17/8/17 To 30/31st/8/17	17/08/1917	17/08/1917
Miscellaneous			
Heading	Cover for Documents. Nature of Enclosures. War Diary of 46th Machine Gun Company from 1st September 1917 to 30th September 1917. Vol 20		
War Diary		01/09/1917	30/09/1917
Miscellaneous	H.Q. 46th L.B.	02/11/1917	02/11/1917
Heading	War Diary Of Machine Gun Company For October 1917 Vol 21		
War Diary		01/10/1917	31/10/1917
Heading	War Diary Of 46th M.G. Company For November 1917 Vol 22		
War Diary		01/11/1917	30/11/1917
Heading	War Diary Of 46th Machine Gun Coy For December 1917. Vol 23		
War Diary		01/12/1917	31/12/1917
Heading	War Diary Of 46th M.G. Company For January 1918. Vol 24		
Miscellaneous	H.Q. 46th L.B.	02/02/1918	02/02/1918
War Diary		01/01/1918	31/01/1918
War Diary	Berneville	01/02/1918	05/02/1918
War Diary	Arras	06/02/1918	28/02/1918

Heading	War Diary Of 46th M.G. Company Vol 25
Miscellaneous	

woos1954 13

15TH DIVISION
46TH INFY BDE

46TH MACHINE GUN COY.
FEB 1916-FEB 1918

46th Bde: M.G. Coy.

Vol: I

46th M.G. Coy
Feb 1/16
Feb 11/16

Army Form C. 2118

WAR DIARY
or
INTELLIGENCE SUMMARY

(Erase heading not required.)

Diary of No "46" Brigade Machine Gun Company

(Feb 7ᵗʰ — Feb 29ᵗʰ)

WAR DIARY
~~INTELLIGENCE SUMMARY~~

(Erase heading not required.)

Army Form C. 2118

Instructions regarding War Diaries and Intelligence Summaries are contained in F. S. Regs., Part II. and the Staff Manual respectively. Title Pages will be prepared in manuscript.

Place	Date	Hour	Summary of Events and Information	Remarks and references to Appendices
Grantham	July 7th	10.30 pm	The Company left Harrowby Camp to entrain at Grantham Station.	
"	" 8th	1 am	The Train left for Southampton	
Southampton	" 8th	9 am	Arrival at Southampton	
"	" 8th	6.30 pm	The Boat left for Havre. The Coy were divided up; the Transport and 60 men under 2/Lt Tunnercom S.S. Courtfield whilst the remainder of the Company under Captain Morrogh left on S.S. Lydia	
Havre	" 9th	7.30 am	S.S. Lydia arrived at point of disembarkation	
"	" 9th	9.30 am	S.S. Courtfield arrived at Havre	
"	" 9th	5 P.m.	Company marched up to No 5 Rest Camp where it was placed under Canvas.	
Havre	11th	9 pm	Camp was left and Company proceeded to Station	

Army Form C. 2118

Instructions regarding War Diaries and Intelligence Summaries are contained in F. S. Regs., Part II. and the Staff Manual respectively. Title Pages will be prepared in manuscript.

WAR DIARY
or
INTELLIGENCE SUMMARY
(Erase heading not required.)

Place	Date	Hour	Summary of Events and Information	Remarks and references to Appendices
Havre	7 Feb 12	12.30 a.m	Train left Havre en route for Noeux-les-Mines	
Noeux les-Mines	" 12	6 pm	Train arrived at destination.	
Mazingarbe	" 13	2 am	Company was billeted in Huts in Mazingarbe.	
"	" 13	4.30 pm	Inspection by Brigadier-General T. G. Matheson	
"	" 14		Billets changed.	
"	" 16	8.30 am	Captain Monagh, 2/Lts Turner, Isaac, Watson and Hamilton visited the Section of Trenches held by Scottish Rifles	
"	" 18	8.30 am	2/Lts Shipley, Nowler, Franklin, and Anderson visited Trenches	
"	" 19 " 20 " 21 " 22		Diggings in Reserve Trenches and Turns at Noeux-les-Mines	

1875 Wt. W593/826 1,000,000 4/15 J.B.C. & A. A.D.S.S./Forms/C. 2118.

WAR DIARY
or
INTELLIGENCE SUMMARY

(Erase heading not required.)

Army Form C. 2118

Place	Date	Hour	Summary of Events and Information	Remarks and references to Appendices
Margate	23rd	8.45 a.m	Sec officers and 3 6 O.R. proceeded to the Trenches. The men were attached in pairs to the guns in the Sector whilst officers were attached to M.G. Section officers.	
"	"	6 pm	Officers left the Trenches 36 O.R. stayed on	
"	24th	6 pm	All Company officers proceeded to Trenches withdraw the relief 58 guns carried out. The Officers and 36 O.R. came out of Trenches with the relieved sections	
"	25th	9.a.m	Company proceeded to Gonay for Musketry.	
Gonay	26th 27th		Musketry	
"	28th		Six gun S emplacements	
"	29th		Musketry.	

Army Form C. 2118

WAR DIARY
~~INTELLIGENCE SUMMARY~~
(Erase heading not required.)

46 M G C
Vol 2

War Diary of No 46 Brigade Machine Gun Company

March 1st — March 31st

WAR DIARY
or
INTELLIGENCE SUMMARY

(Erase heading not required.)

Army Form C. 2118

Place	Date	Hour	Summary of Events and Information	Remarks and references to Appendices
Margate	March 1st	10 A.M.	The Company proceeded by motor bus to Margategate.	
"	2nd	6.30 P.M.	No 1 and 2 Sections took over positions in trenches from No 44 Brigade Machine Gun Coy. 9 guns were in Reserve line; 3, 4 in 65 metre redout and 2 in Northern Sap redout: all were in "14 Bis" Sector.	
"	3rd		Two Sections in trenches.	
"	4th			
"	5th	6.30 A.M.	No 3 and 4 Sections relieved No 1 and 2 Sections in same positions	
"	6		Two Sections in trenches	
"	7		Indirect fire in various points carried out.	
"	8			
"	9	6.30 P.M.	No 1 and 2 Sections relieved No 3 and 4th.	

WAR DIARY or INTELLIGENCE SUMMARY

Army Form C. 2118

Instructions regarding War Diaries and Intelligence Summaries are contained in F.S. Regs., Part II. and the Staff Manual respectively. Title Pages will be prepared in manuscript.

(Erase heading not required.)

Place	Date	Hour	Summary of Events and Information	Remarks and references to Appendices
Mazingarbe	March 10th		Two Sections in Trenches	
"	11th		Indirect fire on various points carried out.	
"	12th March			
"	13th	9.30 p.m.	Coy was relieved by the guns of No 45 Brigade Machine gun Company.	
Noyelles	14th	9 A.M.	Company marched from Mazingarbe to Gosnay.	
Gosnay	15th		Musketry and Machine Gun Training	
"	16th		as in programme supplied by 46th Brigade	
"	17th			
"	18th			
"	19th	10 A.M.	Company proceeded to Mazingarbe by Motor bus.	

Army Form C. 2118

Instructions regarding War Diaries and Intelligence Summaries are contained in F. S. Regs., Part II. and the Staff Manual respectively. Title Pages will be prepared in manuscript.

WAR DIARY
or
INTELLIGENCE SUMMARY
(Erase heading not required.)

Place	Date	Hour	Summary of Events and Information	Remarks and references to Appendices
Mazingarb	19th	6.30 PM	Company took over gun positions in the Hulluch Sector.	
"	20th		One gun was in Support line, one was in Reserve line, one was mounted at Lone Tree Redoubt and six were stored there.	
"	21st		Two Sections and 1 out-section were in the trenches.	
"	22nd		Lines for indirect fire on certain points were laid down, but owing to Winnings batteries no fire cones be carried out.	
"	23rd		One gun was placed in the front line at the Salient in order to traverse enemies lines on the explosion of an expected mine. Gas was promptly fired by the gun haken another place in line at point in old Crater.	
"	24th		Several belts fired in answer to enemies fire on explosion of two small mines. Enemies fire was silenced.	
"	25th		Company was relieved by No 1 Machine Gun Squadron and marched to Neuve Les Mines.	

1875 W.t W593/826 1,000,000 4/15 J.B.C. & A. A.D.S.S./Forms/C. 2118.

WAR DIARY
or
INTELLIGENCE SUMMARY

(Erase heading not required.)

Army Form C. 2118

Instructions regarding War Diaries and Intelligence Summaries are contained in F. S. Regs., Part II. and the Staff Manual respectively. Title Pages will be prepared in manuscript.

Place	Date	Hour	Summary of Events and Information	Remarks and references to Appendices
Neuve les Mines	26th	2 pm.	Company marched to Lyonay.	
Lyonay	27th		Trenches cleaned and repaired.	
"	28th		} Musketry and Machine Gun Shooting	
"	29th			
"	30th			
"	31st			

WAR DIARY
or
INTELLIGENCE SUMMARY

(Erase heading not required.)

Army Form C. 2118

Diary of No 46 Bgde M.G. Coy.
April 1st – 30th

Thornton офts + O.Rs
No 46 Bgde M.G. Coy

Vol 3

Army Form C. 2118

WAR DIARY
or
INTELLIGENCE SUMMARY
(Erase heading not required.)

Instructions regarding War Diaries and Intelligence Summaries are contained in F. S. Regs, Part II. and the Staff Manual respectively. Title Pages will be prepared in manuscript.

Place	Date	Hour	Summary of Events and Information	Remarks and references to Appendices
Gosnay	April 1st	7.30 a.m.	An officer of the Company accidentally shot himself while cleaning his revolver.	
"	"	11 a.m.	Company proceeded to Mazingarbe by Motor Bus.	
Mazingarbe	"	7 p.m.	Company relieved 44th Bde. M.G. Coy. in 1A Bde Sector. Attached to 49th I.B., 16th Division. Sub-sections 3, 4, 5 & 6 in the line – 8 guns in and 4 in 65 Metre Redoubt.	
"	2nd		Billets in Mazingarbe. Indirect fire was carried out each night by guns in the line. Reserve teams carried on with training.	
"	3rd		Billets in Mazingarbe.	
"	4th		Billets in Mazingarbe.	
"	5th	12.30 a.m.	Billets in Mazingarbe. Bombardment of Reserve line followed the blowing up of a mine on the Right. One M.G. in Loos buried twice.	
"	6th		Billets in Mazingarbe.	

Army Form C. 2118

WAR DIARY
or
INTELLIGENCE SUMMARY

(Erase heading not required.)

Instructions regarding War Diaries and Intelligence Summaries are contained in F.S. Regs., Part II. and the Staff Manual respectively. Title Pages will be prepared in manuscript.

Place	Date	Hour	Summary of Events and Information	Remarks and references to Appendices
Mazingarbe	April 7th.	7 p.m.	Billets in Mazingarbe. Inter-divisional Relief carried out. Sub-sections 1, 2, 7 & 8 now in the line.	
"	8th.		Billets in Mazingarbe.	
"	9th.	4 p.m.	Billets in Mazingarbe. Reserve line shelled heavily. Dug outs of two teams fell in - a Sergeant killed, one man wounded, others buried but rescued - suffering from shell shock.	
"	10th.		Billets in Mazingarbe. Reserve Line again shelled - two gunners wounded.	
"	11th.		Billets in Mazingarbe. Relieved by 45 th Bde. M.G. Coy.	
Raimbert.	12th.	2 p.m.	Company came by bus to Raimbert for Corps Rest. During this period, systematic training was carried out.	
"	13th.		Billets at Raimbert.	
"	14th.		Billets at Raimbert.	

1875 Wt. W593/826 1,000,000 4/15 T.R.C. & A. A.D.S.S./Forms/C. 2118.

Army Form C. 2118

WAR DIARY
or
INTELLIGENCE SUMMARY
(Erase heading not required.)

Instructions regarding War Diaries and Intelligence Summaries are contained in F. S. Regs., Part II. and the Staff Manual respectively. Title Pages will be prepared in manuscript.

Place	Date	Hour	Summary of Events and Information	Remarks and references to Appendices
Raimbert	April 15th		Billets at Raimbert.	
"	16th		Billets at Raimbert.	
"	17th		Billets at Raimbert.	
"	18th		Billets at Raimbert.	
"	19th		Billets at Raimbert.	
"	20th		Billets at Raimbert.	
"	21st		Billets at Raimbert. Company Officer visited trenches previous to taking over from 37th Bde M.G. Coy. in the Hohenzollern Sector.	
"	22nd		Billets at Raimbert.	
"	23rd		Billets at Raimbert.	
Vermelles	24th		Company moved from Raimbert to Vermelles entraining at Lillers & detraining at Noeux-les-Mines. Company H.Q. established at the Brewery, Vermelles.	

1875 Wt. W593/826 1,000,000 4/15 T.R.C. & A. A.D.S.S./Forms/C. 2118.

Army Form C. 2118

WAR DIARY
or
INTELLIGENCE SUMMARY
(Erase heading not required.)

Instructions regarding War Diaries and Intelligence Summaries are contained in F.S. Regs., Part II. and the Staff Manual respectively. Title Pages will be prepared in manuscript.

Place	Date	Hour	Summary of Events and Information	Remarks and references to Appendices
Vermelles	April 24th Cont.	3 p.m.	Nos. 2 & 3 Sections relieved guns of 34th Bde. M.G. Coy. in the Hohenzollern Sector. 6 guns in Reserve Trench, 2 in support and 2 in Kispe in Village Line.	
		5 p.m.	Company H.Q. shelled about 5 p.m. — one man slightly wounded.	
"	25th		Billets in Vermelles. Most of the guns in the line carried out indirect fire each night.	
"	26th		Three guns put in Village line with skeleton teams. Vermelles heavily shelled. Warning received from Bde. H.Q. of bombing attack on our front. The Company "stood to."	
"	27th	5.45 a.m.	Warned by Telephone from Bde. H.Q. that Gas attack was being made along 4th & 5th Bde. Front. (Quarry Sector) Pre-arranged Defence Scheme carried out — guns in Village line manned.	
		5.50 a.m.	Lachrymatory shells over Company H.Q. (The Brewery, Vermelles)	
		6.15 a.m.	Thick cloud of gas enveloped us & lasted about an hour. One prisoner passed.	
		7.30 a.m.	Warning of a second gas attack received, but the gas passed north of us.	
		5.30–7.30 a.m.	Company H.Q. heavily shelled. During the Gas attack the guns were either kept firing or the working portions were kept working. In every case this proved satisfactory.	
		7 P.M.	Gas alarm again given. Gas shells sent over near Company H.Q.	
		9 P.M.	Gas again reported opposite Hulluch Sector.	

Army Form C. 2118

WAR DIARY
or
INTELLIGENCE SUMMARY
(Erase heading not required.)

Instructions regarding War Diaries and Intelligence Summaries are contained in F. S. Regs., Part II. and the Staff Manual respectively. Title Pages will be prepared in manuscript.

Place	Date	Hour	Summary of Events and Information	Remarks and references to Appendices
Vermelles.	April 28th.		Billets at Vermelles. Several shells in the Brewery (Coy. H.Q. in the early morning.)	
		9.45 p.m	Gas Alarm - "stood to" - no gas over us.	
		10.45 p.m	"Stand down" received from Bde. H.Q.	
"	29th.	4.30 a.m	Very heavy bombardment - "stood to" - Tear shells fell near Coy. H.Q. - Gas Alarm sounded. The gas which was very severe in the Quarries Sector (just south of us) did not pass over us	
"	30th.		Billets in Vermelles. Enemy fairly quiet all day.	

W. T. Morragh Capt.
O/C 46 Bde M. G. Coy.

1875 Wt. W593/826 1,000,000 4/15 J.B.C. & A. A.D.S.S./Forms/C. 2118.

46. M.G. Coy
Vol 4

WAR DIARY
or
INTELLIGENCE SUMMARY
(Erase heading not required.)

Army Form C. 2118

War Diary of 46th Brigade Machine Gun Company

(May 1st — May 31st)

Army Form C. 2118

WAR DIARY
or
INTELLIGENCE SUMMARY
(Erase heading not required.)

Instructions regarding War Diaries and Intelligence Summaries are contained in F. S. Regs., Part II. and the Staff Manual respectively. Title Pages will be prepared in manuscript.

Place	Date	Hour	Summary of Events and Information	Remarks and references to Appendices
Trenches	May 1st		In direct fire opened out. Our lines heavily shelled.	
Bethune	2nd		Relief was completed by 45th Brigade M.G. Coy and Company proceeded to Bethune	
"	3rd		}	
"	4th		}	
"	5th		} Training at Bethune.	
"	6th		}	
"	7th		}	
"	8th		}	
"	9th		16. O.R. from 46th Brigade attended a course at Company Hdqrs	
"	10th		The Company left Bethune and marked into Noyelles. The a/c & Emplyn were retired in their positions. Twelve guns in the line and 4 in the Village	
Noyelles	11th		The Germans attacked us & back and captured trenches about this point. No guns were ever contained directly but supporting indirect fire was used	

1875 Wt. W593/826 1,000,000 4/15 J.B.C. & A. A.D.S.S./Forms/C. 2118.

Army Form C. 2118

WAR DIARY
or
INTELLIGENCE SUMMARY
(Erase heading not required.)

Instructions regarding War Diaries and Intelligence Summaries are contained in F.S. Regs., Part II. and the Staff Manual respectively. Title Pages will be prepared in manuscript.

Place	Date	Hour	Summary of Events and Information	Remarks and references to Appendices
Mayelles	12th		Routine in Trenches. Overhead fire at night	
"	13th		Routine in Trenches. Overhead fire at night.	
"	14th		46th Brigade counter attacked the Germans. Supporting fire on the Enemy's Support & Reserve lines was carried on throughout the action	
"	15th		Overhead fire at Slag alley etc	
"	16th		Overhead fire at Trolley lines etc behind German lines	
"	17th		A Shell struck one of our emplacements. Sgt Cadwallader, Pte Brown Killed. Three men wounded	
"	18th		2nd/Lt W.S. Ferris wounded in the arm by a rifle bullet. Intersectional relief carried out	
"	19th		Captain Altbrough left on leave to England	
"	20th		Lieut Dunkerly (attached from 10th Scottish Rifles) left to attend a course at Camiers. Systematic fire on invisible Transport lines carried out	
"	21st		Routine in Trenches. Indirect fire at night at fixed targets. Sniping during day at known Spots.	
"	22			

1875 Wt. W593/826 1,000,000 4/15 J.B.C. & A. A.D.S.S./Forms/C. 2118.

WAR DIARY
or
INTELLIGENCE SUMMARY

(Erase heading not required.)

Army Form C. 2118

Instructions regarding War Diaries and Intelligence Summaries are contained in F.S. Regs., Part II. and the Staff Manual respectively. Title Pages will be prepared in manuscript.

Place	Date	Hour	Summary of Events and Information	Remarks and references to Appendices
Noyelles	23rd		Numerous alternative Emplacements were made. Much work carried out in knocking	
"	24th		Emplacements. Indirect fire at night on Selected Targets and Patrol activity	
"	25th			
"	26th			
			45th Company relieved 46th Coy in all their position	
			The Coy proceeded to Bethune for Divisional rest	
Bethune	27th	5.52	Company left Bethune under Special orders and Concentrated at Noyelles	
			Various Emplacements in the Village line and Keeps were occupied – 14 guns employed	
Noyelles	28th		The Company – today at Noyelles (less 14 guns)	
"	29th		The Company stood by at Noyelles (less 14 guns) 2nd Lieut Anderson eff for O.T.C. course at Yonay	
"	30th			
"	31st		The Company (less 14 guns) stood by at Noyelles	

Army Form C. 2118

XV

46. M.G. Coy

Vol 6

WAR DIARY
or
INTELLIGENCE SUMMARY
(Erase heading not required.)

War
Diary
of
46th Brigade Machine Gun Company

(June 1st — June 30th)

W.F. Morrough Capt
o/c 46th M.G. Coy

Place	Date	Hour	Summary of Events and Information	Remarks and references to Appendices

WAR DIARY
or
INTELLIGENCE SUMMARY
(Erase heading not required.)

Army Form C. 2118

Place	Date	Hour	Summary of Events and Information	Remarks and references to Appendices
Nogelles	May 1st		Company stood by at Nogelles with 4 guns in the Village line	
"	2nd		Company stood by at Nogelles with 4 guns in Village line	
"	3rd		Company relieved 44th Company in the Hohenzollern Sector 3 guns were in Support & 5 in the Village line with Shelter teams	
"	4th		Indirect fire on known points was carried out at intervals during the night especially on tracks and roads behind the Dump. There was not much retaliation	
"	5th		Considerable indirect fire was again carried out. The two retaliation was fairly heavy with high explosive	
"	6th		More indirect fire at Road junctions and Tracks in neighbourhood of the Dump	
"	7th		Heavy shelling by an armoured train. Three Nre guns positions from which firing had taken place. One emplacement was knocked in 2nd Lt J.W. Porter joined from Grantham	

Army Form C. 2118

WAR DIARY
or
INTELLIGENCE SUMMARY
(Erase heading not required.)

Instructions regarding War Diaries and Intelligence
Summaries are contained in F. S. Regs., Part II.
and the Staff Manual respectively. Title Pages
will be prepared in manuscript.

Place	Date	Hour	Summary of Events and Information	Remarks and references to Appendices
Noyelles	8th		Emplacement entrance cleared and made ready to use R.E. who were to report it. As another emplacement was being constructed nothing was commenced.	
"	9th		Routine in the trenches. Indirect fire on selected points at night. B.C. Snape left on leave for England.	
"	10th			
"	11th		Intellectual relief	
"	12th			
"	13th		Rest in the Trenches	
"	14th			
"	15th		Indirect fire at night and in some cases by day on numerous B.C.s of special importance. Targets noticed in Intelligence reports engaged as far as possible	
"	16th			
"	17th			
"	18th			
"	19th		Relieved by 45th Brigade H.Q. Company	

WAR DIARY
or
INTELLIGENCE SUMMARY

(Erase heading not required.)

Army Form C. 2118

Place	Date	Hour	Summary of Events and Information	Remarks and references to Appendices
Noyelles	June 20th		Billets at Noyelles. 5 guns in the Village line. Overhauled and clean up of limbers	
	21st		Guns sent to advance stores. All returned with a report that conditions and care of them had been excellent	
	22nd		Billets at Noyelles	
	23rd		Routine in billets at Noyelles and in the Village line	
	24th			
	25th			
	26th			
	27th		Relieved No 46 Company in the Hulluch Sector.	
	28th		Aeroplane fired at but flying too high. Indirect fire at night. Mjr Watson left for England on leave	
	29th		Fairly busy day at Battery positions. Loopholes in dump were engaged. Much indirect fire at night	
	30th		Indirect fire by day and night at selected pts. One man severely wounded, one man suffering from shell shock. A Stokes team in	

15/ July.
46. M.G.C.
vol. 6

Confidential

War Diary 46th M.G. Coy.

From 1st July to 31st July 1916

WAR DIARY
or
INTELLIGENCE SUMMARY

War Diary 46th Brigade M.G. Coy

July 1st —— July 31st

Army Form C. 2118

WAR DIARY or INTELLIGENCE SUMMARY

Army Form C. 2118

(Erase heading not required.)

Instructions regarding War Diaries and Intelligence Summaries are contained in F. S. Regs., Part II. and the Staff Manual respectively. Title Pages will be prepared in manuscript.

Place	Date	Hour	Summary of Events and Information	Remarks and references to Appendices
Noyelles	July 1st		A large number of bombs hurled at various pts behind enemy's lines caused retaliation in the course of which one emplacement dug out was blown in. One OR was killed & two wounded.	
"	" 2		More indirect fire at night. Gas was sent over at Hr 40 approx [?] in front an old communication and dumps. Dug out firing was carried out in enemy's reserve trench South of Hulluch. 1 OR wounded.	
"	" 3		Heavy fire on all enemy communications at also an approach to My emplacement or dump. an (Heavy) battery behind it.	
"	" 4		A Raiding Party entered the enemy's trenches ad headed dugs etc. Prisoners were taken. Before we raid enemy front line was extended and during we raid intense fire was opened on communication trenches and roads.	
"	" 5		Intermittent fire at various pts at night	

WAR DIARY
or
INTELLIGENCE SUMMARY

(Erase heading not required.)

Army Form C. 2118

Instructions regarding War Diaries and Intelligence Summaries are contained in F. S. Regs., Part II. and the Staff Manual respectively. Title Pages will be prepared in manuscript.

Place	Date	Hour	Summary of Events and Information	Remarks and references to Appendices
Noyelles	July 6		Indirect fire on fixed pts	
"	" 7		"	
"	" 8		"	
"	" 9		Indirect fire on fixed pts. Lieut J.S. Dunterley 1050 Rft. left the Company to join the Royal Flying Corps.	
"	" 10		"	
"	" 11		Indirect fire on fixed pts	
"	" 12		and routine work in the Trenches	
"	" 13		The Company was relieved by 4th Bridge M.G. Coy and proceeded to billets in Bethune	
Bethune	" 14		Clean up and inspecting of Limbers. Rft. was served out and checked.	

Army Form C. 2118

Instructions regarding War Diaries and Intelligence
Summaries are contained in F. S. Regs., Part II.
and the Staff Manual respectively. Title Pages
will be prepared in manuscript.

WAR DIARY
or
INTELLIGENCE SUMMARY
(Erase heading not required.)

Place	Date	Hour	Summary of Events and Information	Remarks and references to Appendices
Bethune	15th		Billets at Bethune	
"	16th			
"	17th		Various class	
"	18th		held	
"	19th		at M.G. HQrs	
"	20th			
Bethune	21st		Company left Bethune and marched to Marles-Mines via Gorre. Coy arrived at Marles-les-Mines at 2pm at value. Were billeted for the night. Coy moved with 46th Brigade	
Marles les Mines	22		Company left Marles-Mines and moved via Pernes & Hucheu where they were billeted for the night. Still with Brigade	

WAR DIARY
or
INTELLIGENCE SUMMARY

(Erase heading not required.)

Army Form C. 2118

Place	Date	Hour	Summary of Events and Information	Remarks and references to Appendices
Heuchin	23rd		Billets at Heuchin. Church parade 32 men attended. Whole Company for the Brigade.	
"	24th		Billets at Heuchin.	
"	25th		Billets at Heuchin. The Company practised galloping to action in divers and taking up various positions.	
"	26th		Company left Heuchin at 8 A.M and marched to Blangermont arriving there at 2.30 p.m.	
Blangermont	27th		Company left Billets and marched to Chateau le Bourson near Wavans arriving there at 1.30 p.m.	
Wavans	28th		Company left Billets and marched to Bonnieres Frenchateaux at 4.30 p.m and finished at 12 noon.	
"	29th		Billets at Bonnieres	

Army Form C. 2118

WAR DIARY
or
INTELLIGENCE SUMMARY
(Erase heading not required.)

Place	Date	Hour	Summary of Events and Information	Remarks and references to Appendices
Bermeuil	30th		Billets at Bermeuil. Gun cleaning. Inspecting of limbers, and belt filling. Evening parade.	
	31st		The Company marched to Flesselles, starting at 5 AM and arriving at destination at 8:30 am.	

46th Brigade.
15th Division.

46th BRIGADE MACHINE GUN COMPANY

AUGUST 1 9 1 6

WAR DIARY
or
~~INTELLIGENCE SUMMARY~~

Army Form C. 2118

46 M G C

Vol 7

War Diary of 46th Machine Gun Company

(August 1st – August 31st)

Army Form C. 2118

WAR DIARY
or
INTELLIGENCE SUMMARY

(Erase heading not required.)

Instructions regarding War Diaries and Intelligence Summaries are contained in F.S. Regs., Part II. and the Staff Manual respectively. Title Pages will be prepared in manuscript.

Place	Date	Hour	Summary of Events and Information	Remarks and references to Appendices
Flesselles	Aug 1st		Billets at Flesselles. Training in musketry & skill eta. Special Instructor (attached) Scotchmen.	
"	2nd		Infantry party and clearing. Practice in open warfare. Machine guns in defence.	
"	3rd		Hostile guns in defence in open warfare. Gun learning etc. Two guns were attached to each battalion in the Brigade in a practice attack. No touch to touch.	
Flesselles Hallou in Bois	4th	6.40 A.M.	The Bay. left Flesselles at 4 A.M. and proceeded to Hallou Bois via Nt. Halu Villers through Havre Brigade camping & billets in Bois	
"	5th		The Brigade marched to Franvillers leaving at 4.15 A.M. and arriving at 7.30 A.M. Coy was billeted having no day and ————— nights

1875. Wt. W593/826 1,000,000 4/15 J.B.C. & A. A.D.S.S./Forms/C.2118.

WAR DIARY
or
INTELLIGENCE SUMMARY
(Erase heading not required.)

Army Form C. 2118

Instructions regarding War Diaries and Intelligence Summaries are contained in F.S. Regs., Part II. and the Staff Manual respectively. Title Pages will be prepared in manuscript.

Place	Date	Hour	Summary of Events and Information	Remarks and references to Appendices
Franvillers	6th		The Coy left Franvillers to take up positions in the new defensive line. Began to peter out W. Two guns were placed in a detached tie in Support and two in the Franklers No 1 & 2. action proceeded. Our two maxim guns did not proceed to this line because of an attack on the right.	
Fricourt	7th		Guns in Support ad redoubt were shelled. Two guns went up to the front line.	
"	8th		Guns in front line saw enemy parties crossing in open to their trenches. These were fired on successfully causing many casualties. Retaliation by enemy heavy artillery.	
"	9th		Trenches and gun positions heavily shelled by enemy. Many hits on Support line searched at intervals.	
"	10th		Emplacements were constructed and shelters improved. Short fire from a few guns on enemy working points.	

Army Form C. 2118

WAR DIARY
or
INTELLIGENCE SUMMARY

(Erase heading not required.)

Instructions regarding War Diaries and Intelligence Summaries are contained in F. S. Regs., Part II. and the Staff Manual respectively. Title Pages will be prepared in manuscript.

Place	Date	Hour	Summary of Events and Information	Remarks and references to Appendices
Ficart	Aug. 11th		Guns were able to catch several detached parties of Germans crossing in front of Martinpuich. One big party was dispersed and severely dealt with.	
"	"	10th	An attack was made by Australians, 4th Brigade and 46th Brigade on the German switch line. This succeeded mostly but in front of our Brigade was unsuccessful.	
"	13th		All gun positions very heavily shelled by the enemy but many excellent targets obtained in the early morning when many German men occurred for in endeavouring to reach their shelters. 1 O.R. killed 6 O.R. wounded.	
"	14th		Relief of one section in the trenches. Again enemy in the early morning was seen of German guns and heavy rounds	

WAR DIARY
or
INTELLIGENCE SUMMARY

(Erase heading not required.)

Army Form C. 2118

Place	Date	Hour	Summary of Events and Information	Remarks and references to Appendices
Fricourt	Aug 15th		Our guns saw very few targets in the shape of German patrols but they engaged at intervals aeroplanes which attempted to cross our line	
"	16		Our guns bombarded the enemy trenches very severely at intervals and in consequence retaliatory bombardments caused our guns a certain amount of trouble.	
"	17		Very heavy shelling of all our positions. Guns were all mounted in turn any however, and much enemy was done at wiring German who ran from shell hole to shell hole having his shrewal.	
"	18th		Very heavy bombardment of all our gun positions which caused us many casualties. An enemy counterattack was attempted in the night against some of our advanced position but this was both up by our fire. Our casualties were 4 OR killed 11 OR wounded	

WAR DIARY or INTELLIGENCE SUMMARY

(Erase heading not required.)

Army Form C. 2118

Place	Date	Hour	Summary of Events and Information	Remarks and references to Appendices
Tincourt	19th		The Company was relieved by 45th Machine Gun Company and on relief it proceeded to lines which about where it was bivouaced. Rain was very heavy all day.	
Albert	20th		1 battalion Hun sent by lorried into 3 III Corps M.M.G. School. These and to form an attached reinforcement for the Company. In addition 7 O.R. were sent here from Brigade.	
"	21st		} Bivouac outside Albert. Training for all attached and	
"	22nd			
"	23rd			
"	24th			
"	25th			
"	26th		Refresher Courses on Infantry drill for the Company.	

WAR DIARY or INTELLIGENCE SUMMARY

Army Form C. 2118

(Erase heading not required.)

Place	Date	Hour	Summary of Events and Information	Remarks and references to Appendices
Albert	27th		The Company left its bivouac to take up position in the line between High Wood and Bazentin le Petit. Headquarters were established at Flatiron Wood. No 3 Company were relieved here going into pieces in sap two yds from front line. Two others were in Reserve 300 yds in O.C.1 one in front line, one in Support	
Mametz	28th		Two prisoners of the 133rd Saxons surrendered at the gun position in the sap. Four more Saxons surrendered later in the day. They all appeared well fed & in good health. They state that Saxons are ready to give in at any moment but that the Bavarians will never admit defeat.	
"	29th		Our guns sniped at odd Germans. A German gun was observed in an old trench & it was extracted & out night & proved to be a Russian Machine gun that had been carried [by] us into German ammunition. The enemy shelling was less severe	
"	30		Very heavy shelling in places but on the whole it was slacker. Much rain fell hiring the trenches into a quagmire everywhere.	

Army Form C. 2118

WAR DIARY
or
INTELLIGENCE SUMMARY

(Erase heading not required.)

Instructions regarding War Diaries and Intelligence Summaries are contained in F. S. Regs., Part II. and the Staff Manual respectively. Title Pages will be prepared in manuscript.

Place	Date	Hour	Summary of Events and Information	Remarks and references to Appendices
Nantry	30th		Many new posts were dug for Company & 6 Lewis etc. Lewis Gun teams were instructed the Company guns placed in special position	
"	31st		German aeroplanes flying low were engaged and fired on indirectly with our Lewis gun particulars was taken to make a suitable and watertight dump. gun again used to protect working dugging operations	

1875 Wt. W593/826 1,000,000 4/15 T.R.C. & A. A.D.S.S./Forms/C. 2118.

Army Form C. 2118

Vol 8

WAR DIARY
or
INTELLIGENCE SUMMARY
(Erase heading not required.)

Confidential

46th Machine Gun Company

War Diary

(Sept 1st — Sept 30th)

WAR DIARY or INTELLIGENCE SUMMARY

Army Form C. 2118

(Erase heading not required.)

Instructions regarding War Diaries and Intelligence Summaries are contained in F. S. Regs., Part II. and the Staff Manual respectively. Title Pages will be prepared in manuscript.

Place	Date	Hour	Summary of Events and Information	Remarks and references to Appendices
Sept 1st Mametz Wood	1st		During the day hostile aeroplanes flew over our lines. They were attacked by our Machine guns, otherwise they were unmolested. Indirect fire during the night was placed on the tracks behind High Wood. Our gun in Bethell Sap fired bursts throughout the night at a Snapshot MG emplacement in High Wood. A Bombing attack developed in the night and during this all the ground behind High Wood was swept by our fire. Track Motors & Medium calibre howitzers were brought up by the Germans. One gun was completely destroyed by shell fire.	
"	2nd		Numerous enemy aeroplanes attempted to cross our lines in his direction of Bethell Sap but they were all turned back by our fire. During the night his MG again maintained on the tracks behind High Wood and this gun was completely smashed by shell fire and two teams were buried. Two S.R. were badly wounded as afterwards buried & brought in	
"	3		The first shown on our right made an attack on High Wood. This was successful up to a point but a heavy counter-attack drove us back; he supported this attack with our gun in Bethell Sap, which	

WAR DIARY
or
INTELLIGENCE SUMMARY

(Erase heading not required.)

Army Form C. 2118

Instructions regarding War Diaries and Intelligence Summaries are contained in F.S. Regs., Part II. and the Staff Manual respectively. Title Pages will be prepared in manuscript.

Place	Date	Hour	Summary of Events and Information	Remarks and references to Appendices
Mametz	3rd		Fired over 3,500 rounds between noon and 5.30 pm. The enemy were massed all eveng in retreat and several shell which later parties attempting to reinforce were cut up by m/gun fire and stragglers sniped for a considerable time afterwards. At least 50 germans must have been killed outright during the night. Very much relieved as trenches in Wood	
"	4th		Very heavy shelling by the enemy in wrecklage. 2 damaged guns. 1 still serviceable were marked as they were worn out linears. Suspect had a night in our wood park	
"	5th		The Company was relieved in the line by 101st Machine Gun Company and proceeded to Enely Trench near Fricourt where they were rested in close support of the right sector	
Fricourt	6th		All centers reported well cleared. Guns were overhauled and thoroughly cleaned. Men were clothed and clothing in order. Orders	

1875 Wt. W593/826 1,000,000 4/15. T.B.C. & A. A.D.S.S./Forms/C. 2118.

WAR DIARY
or
INTELLIGENCE SUMMARY

(Erase heading not required.)

Army Form C. 2118

Place	Date	Hour	Summary of Events and Information	Remarks and references to Appendices
In cant	7th		The Coy remained in Support in Shelly Trench as much training as possible was carried on.	
"	8th			
"	9th			
"	10th			
"	11th			
"	12th		The Coy marched to Catalmava and took up position in the line from 108 Brigade. Three guns were placed in Cameron Trench 2 in O&1 and the other were placed in part on instead of 2nd canadian division. Very heavy enemy shelling in our covered block guns were manned but luckily no damage was done, except to one gun.	
Catalmaize	13		An attack was to be made by the Canadian 13th Brigade on 50th Division. A Series of Blyches were down and officers of no Corps proceeded to the trenches to reconnoitre their starting point, on return, Two guns were withdrawn from Catal maize area and Ten guns proceeded to new front System in addition to those already there	
"	14			

1875 Wt. W593/826 1,000,000 4/15 J.B.C. & A. A.D.S.S./Forms/C. 2118.

WAR DIARY or INTELLIGENCE SUMMARY

Army Form C. 2118

Place	Date	Hour	Summary of Events and Information	Remarks and references to Appendices
Contalmaison	15th		The attack was timed for 6.00 A.M. and at this time our machine guns were situated as follows. 3 in Cameron Trench, 2 in O.G.1 & the [sunken] road between & 1 on our [foreign] trench, one in reserve in Gourlay Trench. At 6.20 a.m. with the Right Battalion. 4 with the centre & 3 with the left. Four of these guns went up to proceed to the 1st objective as soon as it was captured & three of them the Sunken Road & one to the outskirts of Martinpuich. Three of these guns managed to reach their objective almost immediately after our infantry had got into the Contalmaison-Martinpuich Road, the team of another gun was knocked out on its way to the Sunken Road. This gun was at once made good by the officer in charge & was [presently] in action made up from a third team from holly Two and named a [Guernsey] gun which had been captured at 6.30 a.m. We guns were ensuring casualties. Two Vickers and one German in Sunken Road — one gun in a shell hole on the outskirts of Martinpuich — 3 in O.G. & our [rifles] (which were [?] [guns] and [?] in Cameron Trench. During the interval between the first and second stages we had two guns [directly] to the left Battalion and great execution on Germans hurrying & retiring from the Sunken Road as we moved North of it. At 9.25 the six guns in shell holes proceeded to the final objective with the Battalion, shortly after the first waves of infantry. At 7.15 a.m. the guns were situated as follows — 6 in factory line (We being with each Battn.) 1 gun southern edge of Martinpuich — 3 (one German) in the Sunken Road — 3 in Cameron Trench — 2 in O.G.1 — 1 in Reserve. After reaching their objectives the guns were at once dug in and ammunition was got up. Up to this time two officers had been put out of action and about 15 men. Three Gunners were made up as soon as possible from Gourlay Trench. Since all reserve men had been used. Before the attaining of the final objective one machine gun was near of the village and three had been wounded leaving only one (found with the guns) at the Cameron Trench. The Officer in Cameron Trench went forward to take up the Right guns in Martinpuich but he was wounded on the way across, After Gourlay Trench had been taken three of our guns [started] in the factory line were [set] across (camouflaged) & were replaced by the three guns in the sunken road. The guns in the Sunken Road were replaced by German guns.

1875 Wt. W593/826 1,000,000 4/15 J.B.C. & A. A.D.S.S./Forms/C.2118.

WAR DIARY
or
INTELLIGENCE SUMMARY

Army Form C. 2118

(Erase heading not required.)

Instructions regarding War Diaries and Intelligence Summaries are contained in F.S. Regs., Part II. and the Staff Manual respectively. Title Pages will be prepared in manuscript.

Place	Date	Hour	Summary of Events and Information	Remarks and references to Appendices
Authuille	13th		Spare men were sent for from Eng H.Qrs. to help to man them. At 10.30 A.M. the guns were situated as follows: 3 in gun pit in head — 3 in Sunken Road — 5 in factory left — 1 in Pilchers of Hornpinch — 3 in Croisilles Trench and O.G.1 — 1 in Reserve — 1 on rep = 19. Each gun had 4,100 rounds with it when it reached its objective and more S.A.A. were sent up at once so that immediately after our guns had reached their objectives they had sufficient ammunition to stand a perfect counter attack. At 4 P.M. the enemy only Captain Murphy and two officers left. At 5 P.M. Lieut Turner who had gone over with us left H.Q. detached moved up to take over a gun of Higgins. He and Lieut Hart up near had remained in charge of guns in the gun pit had knocked out a gun and rifle bombed 12 guns in dug-out. Neither had been seen alive since the three whole days they were in new position. It was also tied to recover their bodies while war was their no relief for them. The attack had been most successful.
"	14th		Returned by 4th Line Brigade. Night spent at bivouac.
"	15th		Company marched to Senlis in pouring rain. The lost 2 sets in new journey. New kits obtained & procured.
Senlis	16th		Company marched to Johnsonny and only make billets in town. Limber guns, etc cleaned.
Johnsonny	17th		Training in Johnsonny
"	18th		"
"	19th		"
"	20th		Company recovered orders and marched to Albert arriving there at 1 P.M.

Report by Lt. T. H. L. Turner
46 M. G. Cy

About 1. a.m on the night 14/15 an Officer from the Canadians with whom we were in touch on our left, came along to Cameron trench, & reported that the enemy were occupying their front line.

I made arrangements for my left gun to enfilade the Canadian front line, & together with another Canadian officer formed a party of about 30 men as a flank

M. G. Report
10/17/9/16

1.

Report on action of
M.Gs. 46 Coy during attack on
15th inst.

Prior to the attack on
MARTINPUICH on the 15th inst
I had five guns in the line.
three in Cameron trench & two
in OG1

& On the night of the 14/15
I put in another ten guns in
the front system.

At 6.a.m on the 15th inst
The M.Gs were situated as
follows.
Two in OG1
Three in Cameron trench

guard for our left. Before this there was considerable bombing on our left, but I did not hear any further disturbance later.

In advancing at 6.20 a.m the Canadian officer & the thirty men came over with my left gun to protect my left flank in case the front line had not been retaken.

W. F. Monagh Corp
O.C. 46 M.G. Coy

after our infantry had got in, & consolidated positions there.

The team with the fourth gun was knocked out, on its way to the sunken. This loss was at once made good by the Officer in charge of the guns, who at once made up a third team from his other two, & manned a German gun which had been captured.

At 6.30. a.m the guns were situated as follows.
Two Vickers & one German in Sunken Road

2.

Ten divided between the front
line & Bacon trench
One in reserve in Gourlay trench

At 6.20 a.m ten guns
went over with the infantry, three
accompanying the right Bn,
four the centre, & three the left.

Four of these guns were
to proceed to the first objective
as soon as it was captured,
three of them to the Sunken Road, &
one to the outskirts of
Martinpuich. Three of these
guns managed to reach their
objectives almost immediately

4.

one in a shell hole on the outskirts of Martinpuich.

Six in shell holes between the first objective & Zieir trench.

During the interval between the first & second attack, the remaining two guns attached to the Left Battn did great execution on the Germans trying to retire from the Bapaume road & the ridge North of it.

At 0.25 hrs the six guns mentioned above proceeded to the final objective with the Battns, & which they reached

very shortly after the first
waves of the Battn.

At 7.15 a.m the guns were
situated as follows

6 guns   Factory Line two being
                  with each Bn

1 gun   Southern end of Martinpuich

3 guns (1 lost)   Sunken Road

3   "   Cameron Trench

2   "   O G 1

1   "   in Reserve

16 Total.

On reaching their objectives the

7.

& one in Cameron trench.
I ordered the officer at Cameron
trench go forward & to take
over the right guns in Martinpuich
& he proceeded to do so, but
was wounded on the way across.

After Gunpit trench had
been taken three of the guns
already in Factory line were
sent forward to consolidate
this trench, & they were
replaced by two guns of ours
& one German from the sunken
road

The guns in the sunken road

6.

guns began to dig in at once & to get up their ammunition supply. Up to this time two officers had been hit & put out of action, & about 15 men

These casualties were made up as soon as possible from Coy hqs at Gourlay trench where I left all my reserve men.

Between the attaining of the final objective, & the ~~order~~ attack on the rest of the village another two officers had been wounded, leaving only one officer forward with the guns

8.

were replaced by German Guns
& Sent forward. Your men from
Coy Hqrs to help to man them.

At 10.30 a.m the guns
were situated as follows.

3	in Gunpit trench
3 (lost)	in Sunken Road
5	Factory line
1	in outskirts of Martinpuich
3	Cameron trench
2	O G 1
1	Lost
1	Blown up.
19	Total.

9

Each gun team had 4100 rounds with it when it reached its objective, & more S.A.A was got up at once, so that immediately after the guns had reached their objective they had sufficient ammunition to withstand a prolonged counter attack.

About By four in the afternoon I had only two officers & myself left. I sent 1st Isaac forward to take over the right group of guns, & he & 2nd Turner who had gone over with the two

guns attached to the left
m for the attack, took command
of the 12 guns in and around
Martinpuich, & remained in charge
of them for the three whole
days they were in that position,
& went round each of the
guns of their group at frequent
intervals of the day & night
in spite of very heavy shell
fire. The men also had to remain
in the whole time as I had no
one to relieve them with.
20/9/16

W. F. McHugh Capt
o/c 46 M. G. Coy

"A" Form.   Army Form C. 2121.
MESSAGES AND SIGNALS.   No. of Message_____

TO { 46th L.B.

Day of Month: 12th

AAA

TM Bty. Hdqrs. X.16.b.6.2. both officers & men: Two mortars in line both at present in Highland Trench, one at either end, map references, X.6.C.8.6. and X.6.a.3.5. From the present positions it is impossible to reach the German line, Bottom Trench. From the front line, or even saps it is also out of range. At present the two mortars are trained on No Man's Land, in front of gaps, in view of a hostile attack. Two other mortars are held in reserve at Hdqtrs. with personnel ready to move at a moment's notice. A forward dump of T.M. amm. is being established at top of Shetland Alley, near No.4 Strongpoint.

From
Place
Time 6.15 P.M.

[signature] Capt.
O.C. Battery

Action of 46th Trench Mortar
Battery, 46th Brigade, during
advance on 15th, 16th and 17th
September 1916.

On evening of 14th-15th September
1916 two 3" Stokes mortars were
emplaced just off Gordon Alley, on
the right about sixty yards apart,
between Bacon & Lives Trenches. Two
hundred and fifty rounds of ammunition
were placed in readiness beside each
mortar emplacement. Map reference
X 6. c. 8. 8 and X 6. c. 8. 8½
{maps Martinpuich Edition B. 1/20,000
and 15th Div. Map. No. 8.a. 1/10000 13.9.16}
  These mortars were ranged
and trained on Sunken Road running
through R 36 c and M 31 D overnight.
This road was reported to be strongly
held: trench with "dugouts" and M.G.
emplacements running parallel to it.
  Two other 3" Stokes mortars under
2nd Lt Marshall & personnel were in
support at X 6. d. 6. 8, ready to move up
should occasion arise. Lt. Brickman
and 2nd Lt. Myles had charge of one
mortar apiece in Gordon Alley.
  Another two 3" mortars Stokes

II

were held in readiness in reserve at Contalmaison Villa, map reference X.11.d.4.8.

Arrangements had been made also for the carrying party (ammunition) to move forward when necessary. Twenty-four carriers under Sgt. Waddington "stood by" at Advanced Brigade Bomb Store, approx. where Gloster Alley and Gordon Alley meet. This carrying party was to proceed straight up Gordon Alley.

At 6.19 AM on 15-9-16 the two mortars in Gordon Alley open rapid and accurate fire on the Sunken Road area, traversing and searching. Firing ceased at 6.21 AM over 90 rounds having been fired. The infantry met no serious opposition in this Sunken Road, and the assistance of these mortars (to tackle & overcome any strong points, M.G. emplacements, etc.) was not required. Meanwhile the mortars "stood by".

Word duly came back

that the attack was progressing well. I ordered two patrols to be pushed out 8.30 A.M. to ascertain just how far our infantry had reached and the general situation, state of trenches, etc. These two patrols reported part of Martinpuich in our possession, our infantry digging in & consolidating and trenches blocked (with dead, wounded, stretcher bearers, carriers etc.) There appeared no need to move just then, and no call was made on the mortars by the infantry.

The carrying parts then got into operation, and brought more ammunition to our original positions in Gordon Alley. This was at 11. A.M. At 12.30 P.M. word was received from B.H.Q. to push forward 2 mortars to the ultimate objective line. This was being done, as at 11.45 A.M. the 2 mortars were advanced to the outskirts of Martinpuich and "dug in" Map reference. M.32.c.1.5. These mortars were for defensive purposes only, and in the event

IV.

of a hostile counter-attack part of Gunpit Trench and the area between Gunpit Trench and factory line could have been barraged. Getting over ammunition was a heavy task, as the enemy shell-fire in this area was very severe and heavy. Two hundred rounds were got over and stacked in large shell holes, near the mortar positions. Unfortunately an enemy shell pitched amongst the ammunition, and destroyed most of it. At this stage several casualties had occurred both in the mortar personnel and the carriers. The ammunition blown up was replaced after considerable difficulty

At 12.45 P.M. I decided to relieve 2nd Lt. Myles and one of the teams. 2nd Lt. Marshall and a fresh team came up from support in Shetland Alley. As the relief was actually being completed — the three officers were standing together discussing the situation generally, along with myself

VI.

placed in convenient shell holes.
In the afternoon 44th T.M.
Bty. 44th Bde Capt. Stewart relieved
my 2 mortars in Gunpit Trench, and
took over mortars.
During the whole operations
mortars were not required, as the infantry carried
all opposition before them.
The personnel of the
battery and also carriers suffered
severely from the heavy shell fire.
Total casualties, three officers
wounded, two men killed fourteen
N.C.Os and men wounded. Four
men sick. Total all ranks. 23.
Trench mortars in this
battle got little scope, and in future
operations I suggest, after the preparatory
bombardment, the mortars are withheld
until such time as the captured
positions are consolidated, or until
such time as they are actually required
to overcome some strong point.

12 Noon 20.9.16. John O. Graham Capt.
O.C. 44th T.M. Bty.

a German shell wounded both Lt. Brickmann and 2nd Lt. Myles severely. 2nd Lt. Marshall was also very slightly hit, but was able to remain with mortar.

There was no call for trench mortars at this juncture, and the afternoon and night were spent getting up ammunition, and making mortar emplacements.

16th — Relief of one team was carried out. Still at M.32.C.1.5. Several casualties from shell fire which was heavy. Advanced to factory line, both mortars, about 10AM. map reference. M.31.b.9.1 and M.32.C.1.10.

17th — Total casualties at this period about 20 all ranks, including 2 officers severely wounded. Advanced to M.25.d. 8.4. Gunpit trench, both mortars. defensive position. Ammunition problem again evident. Continual shell fire buried many boxes. These boxes were

Army Form C. 2118.

Vol 9

WAR DIARY
or
INTELLIGENCE SUMMARY.
(Erase heading not required.)

War Diary
October 1916

46 M.G. Coy

W.F. Monagh Capt
Vol 46 M.G. Coy

Army Form C. 2118.

WAR DIARY
or
INTELLIGENCE SUMMARY

(Erase heading not required.)

Instructions regarding War Diaries and Intelligence
Summaries are contained in F. S. Regs., Part II.
and the Staff Manual respectively. Title pages
will be prepared in manuscript.

Place	Date	Hour	Summary of Events and Information	Remarks and references to Appendices
Oct 1917 Albert	1st		Church Parade. Sorting of duties and cleaning of kit	
Albert	2nd 3rd 4th 5th 6th 7th 8th		Training carried out under Section arrangements. Section shot in range in turns	
Albert	9th		Company left Albert at 9 A.M. and moved into Bivouac. The whole time disembarked in heavy Train which kept suffered severely from the rain.	
	10		Guns cleaned. Tubes inspected and men thoroughly fresh cleaned up and many in preceded effects.	

Army Form C. 2118.

WAR DIARY
or
INTELLIGENCE SUMMARY.
(Erase heading not required.)

Instructions regarding War Diaries and Intelligence Summaries are contained in F. S. Regs., Part II. and the Staff Manual respectively. Title pages will be prepared in manuscript.

Place	Date	Hour	Summary of Events and Information	Remarks and references to Appendices
Dranoutre	11th		Mine improvements effected. Latrines built & Trenches cleared up and reconstructed.	
"	12th		Training of men attached new and fatigues by the Company to Trench work. Refresher work	
"	13th		General clean up and sorting of Kit.	
"	14th		The Company proceeded to the Trenches to take over the Position occupied held by the 44th & 45th Companies. The Headquarters were established at No. Old Mill which is at No. N. end of Petit park. Guns were placed at the North & to South — 3 guns were placed South of Le Sars.	
Kemmel	15th		Very Heavy shelling of all our lines. Two Emplacements Down in N.E. were demolished and a heavy S.S. Brude silled by a shell. 1 O.R. wounded	

T2134. Wt. W708—776. 500000. 4/15. Sir J. C. & S.

WAR DIARY or INTELLIGENCE SUMMARY

Army Form C. 2118.

Place	Date	Hour	Summary of Events and Information	Remarks and references to Appendices
Hebuterne	16		Last night three emplacements were blown in and a few yards into telles pair in. About 1500 rounds were fired along Bapaume Road N14 B 74 and the ground behind this point at Warlencourt was searched. 1 OR killed. 13 Rwounded.	
"	17		Three Enemy Aeroplanes attempted to cross our lines but went down back by our machine gun fire. One gun position was twice flown over and relieved during which we assisted by no gun Barrum on my right. The Butte de Warlencourt was kept under fire — The Trenches N 17 a and 17 b were searched — The Top of the ridge was traversed. Enemy were prevented from ever trying on Butte.	
"	18		At Daybreak a party of them thirty to fifty Germans were dug about by our Machine Gun fire Several were seen to fall. During the day and night Machine Gun fire was maintained as we falling & between the Butte de Warlencourt — The enemy Trenches N17 a and N17 B a —	

Army Form C. 2118.

WAR DIARY
or
INTELLIGENCE SUMMARY.
(Erase heading not required.)

Instructions regarding War Diaries and Intelligence Summaries are contained in F. S. Regs., Part II. and the Staff Manual respectively. Title pages will be prepared in manuscript.

Place	Date	Hour	Summary of Events and Information	Remarks and references to Appendices
Mahipach	18th		The ground between M10 Central and M11 Central 102 killed from shell stock	
Mahipach	19th		The Company was relieved by the 44th and 45th Companies and proceeded to Lonely Trench trench, no last parties arriving at 7:30am on 20th. The Trenches were in a terrible condition being full of water and the air was utterly cold. All men arrived at Tricant in a parched condition who was the rain had destroyed more than half our shelter.	
Tricant	20th			
"	21st		The Company was employed in Lonely Trench French & along up & ready to move up in support of 44th & 45th Companies	
"	22nd			
"	23rd			
"	24th			
"	25th			
"	26th		Have steadily on have been were started	

Army Form C. 2118.

WAR DIARY
or
INTELLIGENCE SUMMARY.
(Erase heading not required.)

Place	Date	Hour	Summary of Events and Information	Remarks and references to Appendices
Tricourt	27th 28th 29th 30th		The Coy was quartered in Tricourt and ready to move forward in support of the 44th & 45th Coys.	
	31		The Coy moved at Tricourt. Prepared to co-operate whenever an Hour's notice in administration.	

W. F. Morrogh Capt
O/c 46 M.G. Coy

War Diary.

116th Machine Gun Coy.

from 1/11/16 to 31/11/16

Army Form C. 2118.

WAR DIARY
INTELLIGENCE SUMMARY.
(Erase heading not required.)

46 B.M.G.Coy

Vol 10

Place	Date	Hour	Summary of Events and Information	Remarks and references to Appendices
	1916			
Lonely Trench Nov 1			Lonely Trench to Millencourt, arrived Millencourt 6 P.M. Good billets.	
Millencourt	" 2		Billets Millencourt - spent the day cleaning up	
"	" 3		Millencourt. Sent No 4 Section to III Corps M.G. Party to be attached for instruction in Anti-Aircraft duties. They went up to near High Wood	
"	" 4		Millencourt. 2/Lieut' Gooch & Notman joined.	
"	" 5		Moved to Hutments in Henencourt Wood. Huts bad	
Henencourt Wood	" 6		Moved to better huts in Henencourt Wood	

Army Form C. 2118.

WAR DIARY
INTELLIGENCE SUMMARY.
(Erase heading not required.)

Instructions regarding War Diaries and Intelligence Summaries are contained in F.S. Regs, Part II. and the Staff Manual respectively. Title pages will be prepared in manuscript.

Place	Date	Hour	Summary of Events and Information	Remarks and references to Appendices
Henencourt Wood	17th to 14th		Remained at Henencourt. Carried out the training programme as submitted to Brigade Headquarters. Relieved N°1 Section with M.M.G. Party by N°2 Section on 9th.	
"	15th		Marched to Naours about 19 miles. Three men fell out but came along close behind the column. Good billets.	
Naours	16th		Billets Naours. Spent the day cleaning up.	
"	17th		Billets Naours. Carried out training programme.	
"	18th		N°3 Section rejoined the boys from III Corps M.M.G. Party. Carried out training. Church Parade.	
"	19th			
"	20th		Inspection by G.O.C. 46th Inf. Brigade	

T2134. Wt. W708-776. 500000. 4/15. Sir J. C. & S.

Army Form C. 2118.

WAR DIARY
or
INTELLIGENCE SUMMARY.
(Erase heading not required.)

Instructions regarding War Diaries and Intelligence Summaries are contained in F.S. Regs., Part II. and the Staff Manual respectively. Title pages will be prepared in manuscript.

Place	Date	Hour	Summary of Events and Information	Remarks and references to Appendices
Meaux	Nov 21st		Carried out programme of work and firing practice	
"	22nd		Tactical schemes with the Brigades and training programme	
"	23rd		" " " " "	
"	24th		Inspection by Army Commander at 3 P.M.	
"	25th		Tactical schemes with Rest 1/8 K.O.S.B. and Training programme	
"	25th		Usual programme. Officers attended lecture by A.S.C. on supplies	
"	26th		Church Parade	
"	27th		Marched to Warley Road Pillbox	

Army Form C. 2118.

WAR DIARY
INTELLIGENCE SUMMARY.
(Erase heading not required.)

Instructions regarding War Diaries and Intelligence Summaries are contained in F. S. Regs., Part II. and the Staff Manual respectively. Title pages will be prepared in manuscript.

Place	Date	Hour	Summary of Events and Information	Remarks and references to Appendices
Warley	Nov 28th		Carried out programme of work. Billets Warley.	
"	29th		Inspection by G.O.C. Divn. Billets Warley.	
"	30th		Carried out usual programme of work. Billets Warley.	

A.W. Nield Bray Capt.
for O.C. 46 M.G. Coy.

46 M G Coy

Army Form C. 2118.

WAR DIARY
or
INTELLIGENCE SUMMARY.
(Erase heading not required.)

Vol XI

Instructions regarding War Diaries and Intelligence Summaries are contained in F. S. Regs., Part II. and the Staff Manual respectively. Title pages will be prepared in manuscript.

Place	Date	Hour	Summary of Events and Information	Remarks and references to Appendices
A.O.			15th Divn	
			Herewith War Diary for December.	
			W.J. Monagh Capt	
			O/c 46 M.G. Coy	

No. 46 MACHINE GUN COMPANY
No: 1
DATE 8/1/17

Army Form C. 2118.

WAR DIARY
INTELLIGENCE SUMMARY.
(Erase heading not required.)

Instructions regarding War Diaries and Intelligence Summaries are contained in F. S. Regs., Part II. and the Staff Manual respectively. Title pages will be prepared in manuscript.

Place	Date	Hour	Summary of Events and Information	Remarks and references to Appendices
Warloy	1916 Dec 1		In Billets at Warloy. Carried out training programme	
"	" 2		Cleaned up billets in the morning. Marched from Warloy to Pecoul Wood	
			in afternoon. Good billets	
Pecoul Wood	" 3		Church Parade	
"	" 4		Inspection of huts by Brigadier General. Gun drill etc as programme	
"	" 5		Carried out usual programme	
"	" 6		Route march in morning. afternoon usual programme	
"	" 7		Carried out training programme as submitted.	

Army Form C. 2118.

WAR DIARY
INTELLIGENCE SUMMARY.
(Erase heading not required.)

Instructions regarding War Diaries and Intelligence Summaries are contained in F. S. Regs., Part II. and the Staff Manual respectively. Title pages will be prepared in manuscript.

Place	Date	Hour	Summary of Events and Information	Remarks and references to Appendices
Ricourt Wood	Dec 8		Carried out training programme. Section firing on 25 yards range crater	
"	9		" " " "	
"	10		Church Parade	
"	11		Carried out training programme	
"	12		" " " "	
"	13		Tactical Scheme. Prepared for going into trenches	
"	14		Cleaned up billets at Ricourt Camp. Marched from Ricourt Camp to Tranxx Camp. Relieved 14th Boy in the line around and to the right	

T2134. Wt. W708—776. 500000. 4/15. Sir J. C. & S.

Army Form C. 2118.

WAR DIARY
INTELLIGENCE SUMMARY.
(Erase heading not required.)

Instructions regarding War Diaries and Intelligence Summaries are contained in F. S. Regs., Part II. and the Staff Manual respectively. Title pages will be prepared in manuscript.

Place	Date	Hour	Summary of Events and Information	Remarks and references to Appendices
	1916			
of Martinpuich	Dec 14		Coy's Headquarters at Pioneer Camp Contalmaison	
	15		Relieved the remainder of 11th Coy in the line, 6 guns in, 3 in Martinpuich and 4 in Pioneer Camp	
	16		In the line Indirect fire carried out on enemies lines and communications	
	17		" " " " " "	
	18		" " " " " "	
	19		" " " " " "	
	20		" Moved up two guns into posts to E" of Martinpuich	
	21		" " " " " "	
	22		" Indirect fire carried out on enemies lines and communications	
	23		Relieved in the line by 175 M.G. Coy. & took over at Shelter Wood Camp from them. Camp quite comfortable.	
Shelter Wood Camp	24 to 26		In huts at Shelter Wood Camp	

Army Form C. 2118.

WAR DIARY
of
INTELLIGENCE SUMMARY.
(Erase heading not required.)

Instructions regarding War Diaries and Intelligence Summaries are contained in F. S. Regs., Part II. and the Staff Manual respectively. Title pages will be prepared in manuscript.

Place	Date	Hour	Summary of Events and Information	Remarks and references to Appendices
	1916			
	Dec 25		Took over in the sector of the line left of Le Sars from 4th Bry. 4 Guns forward, 2 in posts and 2 in dug-outs.	
	26 to 31		In the line. Indirect fire carried out on enemies lines and communications	

W. F. Morrogh Capt.
4e 46 M. J. Co.

Army Form C. 2118.

WAR DIARY
or
INTELLIGENCE SUMMARY.
(Erase heading not required.)

46 M G Coy

Vol/2

Instructions regarding War Diaries and Intelligence Summaries are contained in F. S. Regs., Part II. and the Staff Manual respectively. Title pages will be prepared in manuscript.

Place	Date	Hour	Summary of Events and Information	Remarks and references to Appendices
H Q			15th Bury	
			Herewith please find War Diary for Jany 1917	
			W.F. Morrogh Capt	
			o/c 46 M G Co	

No 46 MACHINE GUN COMPANY
DATE 31.1.17

T2134. Wt. W708—776. 500000. 4/15. Sir J. C. & S.

Army Form C. 2118.

WAR DIARY
INTELLIGENCE SUMMARY.
(Erase heading not required.)

Place	Date	Hour	Summary of Events and Information	Remarks and references to Appendices
	1917 Jan 1st		In the left sector of the line N.W. of Le Sars. Four guns in the front line, two in coys posts and two in support in a dug-out. Remainder of Company at Acid Drop Camp.	
	2/3		Ditto.	
	4th		Relieved in the line by 45th Coy. Two men wounded while coming out. Returned to Shelter Wood Camp.	
	5/6/7th		At Shelter Wood Camp. Spend the time in cleaning up and improving the Camp.	

Army Form C. 2118.

WAR DIARY
or
INTELLIGENCE SUMMARY.
(Erase heading not required.)

Instructions regarding War Diaries and Intelligence Summaries are contained in F.S. Regs., Part II. and the Staff Manual respectively. Title pages will be prepared in manuscript.

Place	Date	Hour	Summary of Events and Information	Remarks and references to Appendices
	Jan 9th		Relieved 4th Bny in the line to S.E. of Le Sars. Six guns in front system, four in cotton posts, two in Martinpuich. Remainder of the Company at Bivouac Camp. We were very heavily shelled while coming through Martinpuich but had no casualties	
	10th/11th		In the line. Erected an anti-aircraft post	
	12th		One man wounded	
	13th/15th		In the line	

WAR DIARY
or
INTELLIGENCE SUMMARY.
(Erase heading not required.)

Army Form C. 2118.

Place	Date	Hour	Summary of Events and Information	Remarks and references to Appendices
	Jan 16th		Relieved in the line by 45th Bompy and returned to Shelter Wood Camp.	
	17th/19th		At Shelter Wood Camp. Spent the time in cleaning up	
	20th		Relieved 44th Bay in the line N.W. of Le Sars. Five guns in front system, and three in corps posts	
	21st/23rd		In the line	
	24th		Inter-company relief	

Army Form C. 2118.

WAR DIARY
or
INTELLIGENCE SUMMARY.
(Erase heading not required.)

Place	Date	Hour	Summary of Events and Information	Remarks and references to Appendices
	Jan 25th / 26th		In the line. Relieved on 26th by 4/5th L. Infantry and returned to Shelter Wood Camp	
	29th / 30th		At Shelter Wood Camp. Spent the time in cleaning up and preparing to move to Albert	
	31st		Moved from Shelter Wood Camp to Albert	

Army Form C. 2118.

WAR DIARY
or
INTELLIGENCE SUMMARY.

46 M G Coy

Vol 13

(Erase heading not required.)

Instructions regarding War Diaries and Intelligence Summaries are contained in F.S. Regs., Part II. and the Staff Manual respectively. Title pages will be prepared in manuscript.

Place	Date	Hour	Summary of Events and Information	Remarks and references to Appendices
Headquarters				
15th Divn				
			Herewith please find War Diary for Feb 1917	

W.T. Massey? Capt
? ? ? Coy

No 46 MACHINE GUN COMPANY
No.
DATE

Army Form C. 2118.

WAR DIARY
INTELLIGENCE SUMMARY.
(Erase heading not required.)

Instructions regarding War Diaries and Intelligence Summaries are contained in F.S. Regs., Part II. and the Staff Manual respectively. Title pages will be prepared in manuscript.

Place	Date	Hour	Summary of Events and Information	Remarks and references to Appendices
ALBERT	Feb 1st		In billets at Albert, spent the time in cleaning up men and material, checking stores etc	
"	4th			
"	4th		Moved from Albert to Warloy	
WARLOY	5th		In billets at Warloy. Carried out training programme as submitted	
"	6th/7th		Carried out training programme	
"	8th		Route march as per programme. Physical Training under Army Gymnastic Instructor	

Army Form C. 2118.

WAR DIARY
or
INTELLIGENCE SUMMARY.
(Erase heading not required.)

Instructions regarding War Diaries and Intelligence Summaries are contained in F. S. Regs., Part II. and the Staff Manual respectively. Title pages will be prepared in manuscript.

Place	Date	Hour	Summary of Events and Information	Remarks and references to Appendices
WARLOY	Feb 9th/104		Carried out training programme	
"	11th		Church Parade	
"	12th		Carried out training programme	
"	13th		Moved from Warloy to Beauval	
BEAUVAL	14th		" Beauval to Gezaincourt	
GEZAINCOURT	15th		" Gezaincourt to Bonnières	
BONNIERES	16th		" Bonnières to Villers-Sir-Simon	
VILLERS SIR-SIMON	17th		In billets at Villers-Sir-Simon	

Army Form C. 2118.

WAR DIARY
or
INTELLIGENCE SUMMARY.
(Erase heading not required.)

Instructions regarding War Diaries and Intelligence Summaries are contained in F. S. Regs., Part II. and the Staff Manual respectively. Title pages will be prepared in manuscript.

Place	Date	Hour	Summary of Events and Information	Remarks and references to Appendices
VILLERS-SIR-SIMON	Feb 18th		Carried out training programme.	
"	19th/21st		"	
"	22nd		Moved from VILLERS-SIR-SIMON to ARRAS.	
ARRAS	23rd		Relieved 36th Bty in the line and took over 6 guns.	
"	24th		In the line, situation quiet.	
"	25th		" Moved into new billets with Headquarters at	
"	"		51 RUE DE DOUAI	
"	26th/28th		In the line. Supported the attack of the Brigade on our right firing 5,000 rounds indirect overhead fire	

Army Form C. 2118.

46 M.G. Coy

Vol 14

WAR DIARY
or
INTELLIGENCE SUMMARY.
(Erase heading not required.)

A.G.
15th Divn.

Herewith War Diary for March 1917

Army Form C. 2118.

WAR DIARY
or
INTELLIGENCE SUMMARY.
(Erase heading not required.)

Place	Date	Hour	Summary of Events and Information	Remarks and references to Appendices
ARRAS	Mar 1st		In the line. (1"3 Sector) 6 guns in support line	
"	2		Guns in the line relieved by 45th Bgy.	
"	"		Left ARRAS for NOYELLETTE, Lieut. O.H.H. Gray took over command of Bgy. in place of Capt Morrogh (a/Div. Machine Gun Officer)	
NOYELLETTE	3		In billets at NOYELLETTE.	
"	4		Carried out programme of work	
"	5	"	Fitting & testing small box respirators.	
"	6	"	Carried out programme of work. One section firing on range	
"	7			

Army Form C. 2118.

WAR DIARY
or
INTELLIGENCE SUMMARY.
(Erase heading not required.)

Place	Date	Hour	Summary of Events and Information	Remarks and references to Appendices
NOYELLETTE	Mar. 7		In quarry	
"	8th		Route March as programme submitted	
"	9th		返 Carried out training programme	
"	10th		Left NOYELLETTE for GOUY-EN-TERNOIS	
GOUY-EN-TERNOIS	11th		In billets at GOUY-EN-TERNOIS.	
"	12th		Training as programme	
"	13th/14th		Relieved 2 guns of 45th Bay. at L 10 Central (anti-aircraft work)	
"	15th		Engaged in Brigade Tactical Exercise.	

Army Form C. 2118.

WAR DIARY
or
INTELLIGENCE SUMMARY.
(Erase heading not required.)

Instructions regarding War Diaries and Intelligence Summaries are contained in F. S. Regs., Part II. and the Staff Manual respectively. Title pages will be prepared in manuscript.

Place	Date	Hour	Summary of Events and Information	Remarks and references to Appendices
GOUY-EN-TERNOIS	MAR. 16th		Carried out programme of work.	
"	17th		Engaged in Brigade Tactical Exercise.	
"	18th		Left GOUY-EN-TERNOIS for ARRAS.	
ARRAS	19th		In billets at ARRAS. Relieved guns in the line held by 45th Bty	
"	20th/22nd		In the line. Carried out indirect firing on enemy trenches and on gaps in enemy wire. Work done on barrage position.	
"	23rd		Inter company relief. Indirect firing carried out as above.	
"	24th/31st		Indirect firing carried out on enemy trenches & on gaps in enemy wire.	

Army Form C. 2118.

WAR DIARY
or
INTELLIGENCE SUMMARY.
(Erase heading not required.)

Place	Date	Hour	Summary of Events and Information	Remarks and references to Appendices
ARRAS	MAR 24th/31st		Work carried out on bivouac position. 1 O.R. killed on 30th inst. by shell fire. During this time the No. of guns in the line was increased to 10.	
	31		Relieved in the line by 44th bdy in the right sub-sector and	
	"		by 45th bdy in the left sub-sector.	

A.H.H. S. Smyth
O.C. 36 Bty.

WAR DIARY
or
INTELLIGENCE SUMMARY.
(Erase heading not required.)

Army Form C. 2118.

Place	Date	Hour	Summary of Events and Information	Remarks and references to Appendices
H-Q 5th Divn.			Herewith War Diary for April 1917 W.F. Mouaught Capt O/c 46 M.G. Coy	

Stamp: No. 46 MACHINE GUN COMPANY — DATE 2/5/17

Army Form C. 2118.

WAR DIARY
of
INTELLIGENCE SUMMARY.
(Erase heading not required.)

Instructions regarding War Diaries and Intelligence Summaries are contained in F.S. Regs., Part II. and the Staff Manual respectively. Title pages will be prepared in manuscript.

Place	Date	Hour	Summary of Events and Information	Remarks and references to Appendices
April	ARRAS	1st	Capt Morrogh took over 8 barrage guns in the line.	
	DUISANS	2/5th	Remainder of company in billets at DUISANS. Carried out training programme as submitted, in preparation for the attack	
	ARRAS	6th	Remainder of company, (except personnel in reserve) moved to billets in cellars at ARRAS (GRANDE PLACE) with 8 guns.	
	"	7/8th	In cellars at ARRAS. Transport taken over by Brigade T. Officer	
	"	8th	Night of 8th & 9th. Two guns attached to 12th H.L.I.	
	"		" " " 10th Sco. Rifles	
	"		" " " 1/8th K.O.S.B.	
	"	9th	For the attack on April 9th, the guns of 16th M.G. Coy. were allotted as follows:-	

WAR DIARY
INTELLIGENCE SUMMARY.
(Erase heading not required.)

Army Form C. 2118.

Place	Date	Hour	Summary of Events and Information	Remarks and references to Appendices
OPERATIONS.			6 guns creating a machine gun barrage under the division. 2 guns attached to each of the 3 attacking battalions, and 2 in reserve with the reserve battalion 10/11th A.I.F. The guns attached to battalions all joined their respective battalions before they left the bivouac for the blue line. 2/Lieut. R. E. Notman with the 2 guns attached to the 10th A.I.F proceeded with the battalion towards the blue line which was found to be held. During the heat of the battalion before the blue line, ran into it advanced these guns kept up a steady fire on the enemy's trench on the check of the parapet of which they obtained splendid observation, and prevented the enemy infantry and machine gunners firing on our troops. When the battalion advanced to the intermediate line, these guns went with it, and were able to open fire with every gun never in silence in several	

WAR DIARY
INTELLIGENCE SUMMARY.
(Erase heading not required.)

Army Form C. 2118.

Place	Date	Hour	Summary of Events and Information	Remarks and references to Appendices
			parties of the enemy who were seen, and also on HIMALAYA TRENCH. 2/St R.E. Notman and 2/St Gorman (12th N.F.J) then proceeded forward to the BROKEN MILL, and seeing no traces of the enemy, the 2 guns and a boy of the N.F.J took up an advanced position at the MILL in shell holes. From here the guns were able to fire on HIMALAYA TRENCH, and cover the infantry advance. They also fired on some parties of the enemy. After the brown line was captured, these guns took up their position in HIMALAYA TRENCH. The two guns under 2/St. Brown attached to the 7/6th K.O.S.B. got no opportunities for firing until they reached HIMALAYA TRENCH, but opened fire from there on some enemy in the RAILWAY CUTTING and inflicted casualties on them. The two guns attached to the 10th K.O. Rifles and 10/11th N.F.J got no opportunities for firing. After the capture of the brown line, the positions of the M.G's were as follows :- 2 guns EAST of ARRAS. G.23.c	

Army Form C. 2118.

WAR DIARY
or
INTELLIGENCE SUMMARY.
(Erase heading not required.)

Instructions regarding War Diaries and Intelligence Summaries are contained in F. S. Regs., Part II. and the Staff Manual respectively. Title pages will be prepared in manuscript.

Place	Date	Hour	Summary of Events and Information	Remarks and references to Appendices
			6 guns in HIMALAYA TRENCH.	
			2 " " HOKOY LANE.	
			The guns remained in these positions until the night 10/11th. About 10 P.M. on the night 10/11th six of the 8 guns in G.23 c relieved the guns of 4th Coy in HIMALAYA TRENCH. As at midnight night of 10/11th the M.G.'s were situated as follows.	
			2 M.G.'s attached to 31st Divn	
			1 " " out of action from shell	
			13 " " in HIMALAYA TRENCH	
			About 3.45 A.M. orders were received to attack the green line to the North and East of MONCHY-LE-PREUX. On receipt of orders, 2 guns under 2/Lt. W J Brown were attached to the 11th K.O.S.B's and 2 under 2/Lt. L Farquhar to the 10/11th H.L.I. These guns were ordered to take up positions at once on ORANGE HILL, which they did, and to cover the advance of the infantry as far as possible. These guns were not able to render the infantry	

A5834 Wt. W4973/M687 750,000 8/16 D. D. & L. Ltd. Forms/C.2118/13

WAR DIARY
or
INTELLIGENCE SUMMARY.
(Erase heading not required.)

Army Form C. 2118.

Place	Date	Hour	Summary of Events and Information	Remarks and references to Appendices
			any advance during the day, as owing to bad light, it was impossible to distinguish between our own men and the Germans. The guns attached to the 7/8th K.O.S.B's & 10/11th H.L.I, did not reach their orders to join their battalions in time to get in touch with them before the advance began, but they followed the battalions through to MONCHY and got in touch with them there. The two guns with the 10/11th H.L.I went through the village and took up positions east of the village, firing towards PELVES. The two guns with the 7/8th K.O.S.B succeeded in getting into position east of MONCHY, but one gun and limber teams were knocked out later in the day. At 12. NOON. the M.G's were situated as follows :- 4 guns east of MONCHY in shell-holes 9 " " on the forward slopes of ORANGE HILL 2 " " with the 37th Divn 1 " " out of action	

Army Form C. 2118.

WAR DIARY
INTELLIGENCE SUMMARY.
(Erase heading not required.)

Instructions regarding War Diaries and Intelligence Summaries are contained in F. S. Regs., Part II. and the Staff Manual respectively. Title pages will be prepared in manuscript.

Place	Date	Hour	Summary of Events and Information	Remarks and references to Appendices
ARRAS	April 12		About 6 P.M. the two guns remaining in MONCHY were relieved by 111th Brigade and about 3:30 A.M. the guns on ORANGE HILL by the 17th Divn. On relief the guns returned to FEUCHY.	
"	14		During all the operations the greatest difficulty was experienced in trying to get the infantry carrying parties to treat it.	
			Company returned to billets in ARRAS.	
	15/20		Company moved from ARRAS to DUISANS.	
DUISANS			In billets at DUISANS. Carried out training programmes as submitted. Inspection by Brigadier-General on 16th.	
			" C.M.G.O " 19th.	
"	21		Company left DUISANS for ARRAS. (H.Q's 9 RUE DES QUATRE GROSSES) on the evening of the 21st, company went into the line (except personnel in reserve who remained in ARRAS)	

Army Form C. 2118.

WAR DIARY
INTELLIGENCE SUMMARY.
(Erase heading not required.)

Place	Date	Hour	Summary of Events and Information	Remarks and references to Appendices
OPERATIONS.			**FIRST PHASE.**	
			The 16 guns of the company moved into the line on the night of the 21/22nd April, and took up positions as follows :—	
			1 GROUP. 4 guns about N.16.d 7.15 under Lieut A. Hamilton & Lieut A.D. Vaughan	
			2 " 4 " " N.19 a 9.5 under 2/Lieut G.D. de Sieme	
			3 " 8 " " N.11 d 2.5 under Lieut J.N.D. Rocher & 2/Lieut S. Farquhar & Lieut W.S. Gooch	
			from which to cover the advance of the division with a machine gun barrage. The time from their arrival in the line until zero was occupied in making gun emplacements, and getting up ammunition.	
			At 4.45 A.M. on 23/4/17 all guns opened fire on their barrage lines, commencing to lift and search backwards at the rate of 100 yards in 3 minutes, and ceasing fire at the following times.	
			LIFT. CEASE FIRE.	
			1 GROUP: Zero + 3. Zero + 16	
			2 " Zero + 12 Zero + 30	
			3 " Zero + 4 Zero + 24	

WAR DIARY
INTELLIGENCE SUMMARY

The barrage worked perfectly and apparently caused the enemy much annoyance as although the machine guns were situated behind where the enemy dropped his barrage, after they had been firing for about 5 minutes, he seemed to locate their position, and shelled No's 2 & 3 guns heavily, causing several casualties.

At zero + 1 hour the guns moved forward, each officer moving independently with his guns, to Km and Klein at positions as previously chosen, on a line running North & South through O.7.a.2.0. from which to cover the front of the division while consolidating the first objective, and to assist the second attack.

I had fixed on zero + 1 hour as the time for the advance to the second position, as according to programme, by that time our own tanks would have nearly reached their objective, and he will put our second position, I had formed by previous experience that if we have to wait until news came back that the objective has been taken, it would probably be several hours after the infantry have entered the line, before we should be in a position to support them in case of counter attack.

WAR DIARY or INTELLIGENCE SUMMARY

Army Form C. 2118.

No 1 Gun under Lieut. A. Armillan of first at D Vaughan moved forward to Kennel about N.12.c.4.2. from there Lieut. Hamilton went forward to reconnoitre and found that our attack had been held up and that our troops were back in our front line again on that there were 120 or so guns in the front line and also a belonging to 14th and 2 to 45th M.G.Coy Lieut. Hamilton then devised to keep his guns under cover temporarily in a gun pit about N.11.d.1.7 and came abroad on about 1J quite approved of his action.

No 2 Gun under Lieut. G.D. Le Lievre moved forward ≡ at 5.45 A.M. to about N.12.c.5.3. where he learnt that the attack had been driven back and that the 11th A.&S. Highlanders were holding the chalk trench running along SPEAR LANE. He then pushed forward his gun into this trench with the Lewis gun about N.12.c.7.0. and the left about N.12.c. & D. from where a lot of assistance could be given to our own infantry by direct fire. A considerable number of german infantry were observed in numbers

WAR DIARY
INTELLIGENCE SUMMARY
(Erase heading not required.)

Army Form C. 2118.

Instructions regarding War Diaries and Intelligence Summaries are contained in F. S. Regs., Part II. and the Staff Manual respectively. Title pages will be prepared in manuscript.

Place	Date	Hour	Summary of Events and Information	Remarks and references to Appendices
			N.18.c.55.8, holding a strong point and a communication trench running south to GUEMAPPE and a large number were seen running from shell-hole to shell-hole, all these targets were engaged with the guns and all not actually under cover were put out of action.	
			No 3 gun (a) under Lieut J N D Roche advanced at 5.45 A.M. to about N.12.d.4.2 and from there to our own front line when living within to advance further as our own troops had been driven back, then remained, taking advantage of all targets offered.	
			No 3 gun (b) under Lieut L Farquhar & Lieut W S Gosh advanced at 5.45 A.M. and worked our own front line about N.12.c.9.3 and found that our infantry were in shell-holes, being held up in front of GUEMAPPE by a large body of germans, estimated at about 200 in a trench about N.18.b.1.0. They immediately got their guns mounted and opened fire on the enemy here.	
			The ground was perfectly dry and observation of the strike of the bullet	

Army Form C. 2118.

WAR DIARY
or
INTELLIGENCE SUMMARY.
(Erase heading not required.)

Place	Date	Hour	Summary of Events and Information	Remarks and references to Appendices
			perfect, so that the result of the shooting could be easily seen. From their position they enfiladed the trench in which the Germans were, and after about three minutes intense fire they forced the Germans out of their trench. The Germans then tried to run back to GUEMAPPE but as there machine guns were still inflicting heavy casualties on them, they turned round and held up their hands, and surrendered to the attacking battalion of the 44th Inft. Bigde, who had at once commenced to advance again. The strength left of this party when they were forced to surrender is estimated at about 150. The action of these machine guns contributed largely to the capture of GUEMAPPE, which was taken shortly after this. These four guns then tried to advance to the position originally chosen as the 2nd position, about O.7.c.2.2. but were unable to, as our own infantry had been driven back. At 7 A.M. the guns were situated as shown on attached map "A"	

WAR DIARY
or
INTELLIGENCE SUMMARY.

Army Form C. 2118.

(Erase heading not required.)

Place	Date	Hour	Summary of Events and Information	Remarks and references to Appendices
			and remained in these positions until the attack of the 46th Inf. Bgde. in the afternoon. Up to that time (6 P.M.) the company had had 10 casualties. When orders were received for the attack by the 46th Infy. B'gde at 6 P.M. 23/4/19, the guns were situated as shown on the attached map "A". Two guns were attached to each of the attacking battalions, to be under the orders of the O/C battalion. Six were left in SPEAR LANE to cover the advance of the infantry; all these six guns had orders to report to their battalions, as they went through them. The two guns with the 10/11th H. L. I. were ordered to remain in their original position, which they did. The other four advanced with their battalions to about the line of SHOVEL TRENCH, and remained there, and dug positions there. At 8 P.M. night of 23rd. the guns were situated the same as at 7 A.M. with the exception of four guns on a line about O.13.a.6.1. to O.7.c.9.0. During the night these guns were heavily shelled and suffered several casualties.	

SECOND PHASE.

On the morning of the 24th, we received orders to attack the blue line again. Two guns were attached to the 12th H.L.I and 10th Sco. Rifles. Six guns remained in their original positions near SPEAR LANE to keep up a machine gun barrage which was formed across the divisional front on a line running north and south through N.14.a.7.0.

Besides the 6 guns of the 46th M.G. Coy employed on barrage, six out of the eight from each of the 44th & 45th M.G. Coy's (attached to us) were also used for the same purpose.

All the 18 barrage guns opened fire at 4 P.M. searching backwards & forwards at the rate of 100 yards in three minutes until they reached a line running north & south through N 15 a 5.0. ceasing fire about 4.30 P.M. but being prepared to put down a barrage on the same line at once in case of a counter attack.

Two guns of the 45th M.G. Coy were attached to the 11/8th K.O.S.B. and two of the 44th M.G. Coy to the 8/10th Gordons.

Army Form C. 2118.

WAR DIARY
or
INTELLIGENCE SUMMARY.
(Erase heading not required.)

Place	Date	Hour	Summary of Events and Information	Remarks and references to Appendices
			The four guns of the 46th M.G.Coy attached to the 10th Sco. Rifles and 12th H.L.I. remained in SHOVEL TRENCH from where they were able to cover the advance by direct overhead fire. During the attack, these guns did some very excellent work. They located an enemy machine gun and snipers on the ridge at O.9. b. 5.0. which were firing at our troops. They opened fire on them and silenced the machine gun and snipers inflicting many casualties. They were however very heavily shelled, one gun being blown up, and the other completely buried. The buried gun was dug out, found not to be seriously damaged and got into action again. By this time, these four teams had only 13 men left out of 32, but they managed to keep 3 guns in action. As soon as possible, I reinforced these teams by 5 men. The attached maps "B" & "C" show the position of the machine guns after the attack at 6 P.M. on the 23rd, and before and after the attack on the 24th.	

Army Form C. 2118.

WAR DIARY
or
INTELLIGENCE SUMMARY.
(Erase heading not required.)

Place	Date	Hour	Summary of Events and Information	Remarks and references to Appendices
	April 26th		4 guns in the line relieved by 45th Coy.	
	27th		remainder of company in the line relieved by 167th Coy.	
	28th		Company left ARRAS for DUISANS.	
	28th / 30th		In Billets at DUISANS. Spent the time in cleaning guns, checking stores, etc.	

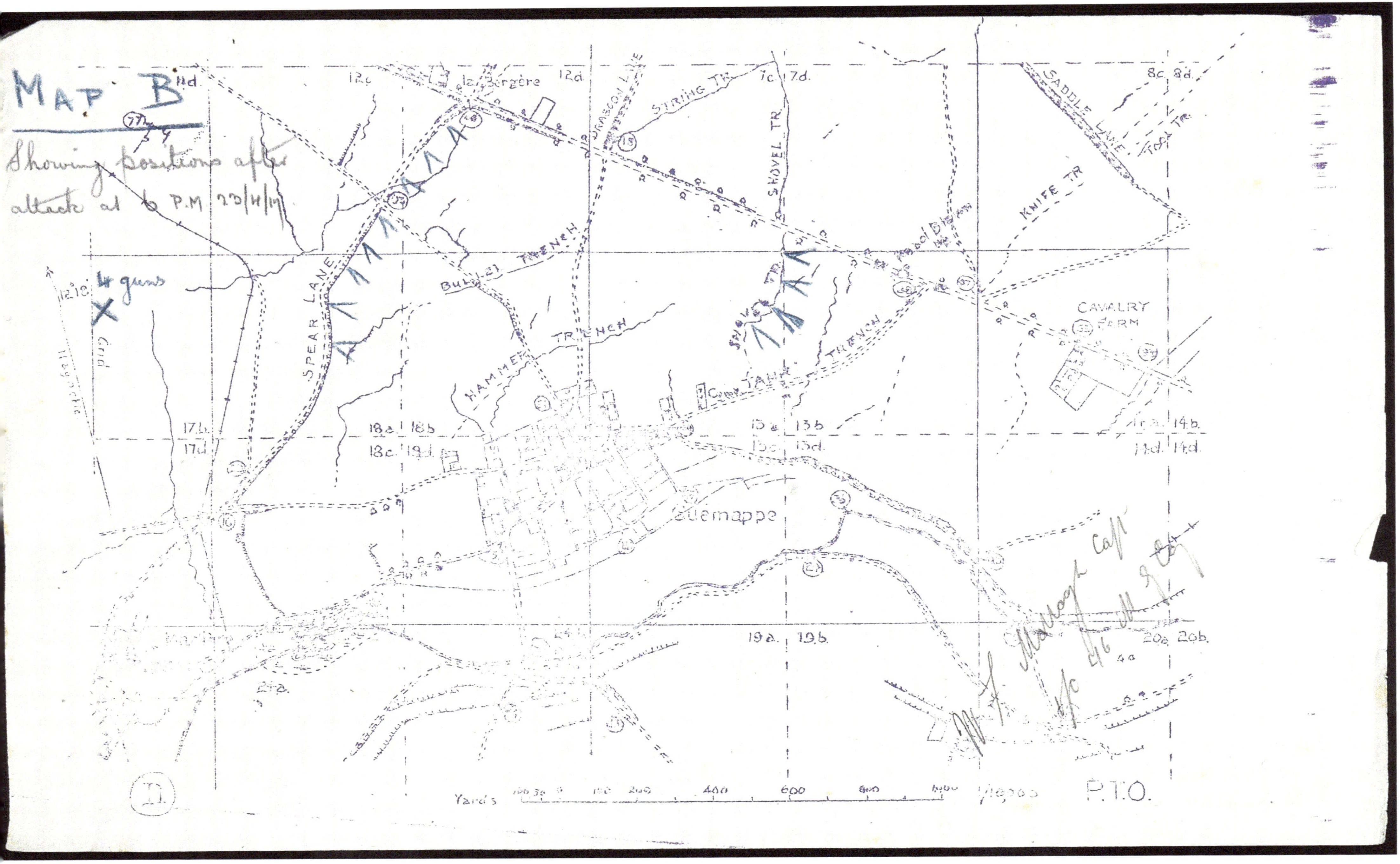

MAP B
Showing positions after attack at 6 P.M 23/4/17
4 guns
Grid
Magnetic
Bergère
SPEAR LANE
BULLET TRENCH
HAMMER TRENCH
DRAGON LANE
STRING TR
SHOVEL TR
KNIFE TR
SADDLE LANE
TOOL TR
CAVALRY FARM
Guémappe
Yards
100 50 0 100 200 400 600 800 1000
1/10,000
P.T.O.

Report. No

From ------------------

To ------------------

Date ------------------

Time ------------------

Am at ------------------
(mark on map)

In touch on } ------------------
right with

In touch on } ------------------
left with

Enemy withdrawing
to ------------------

Enemy massing at ------------------

Remarks ------------------

(Signature) ------------------

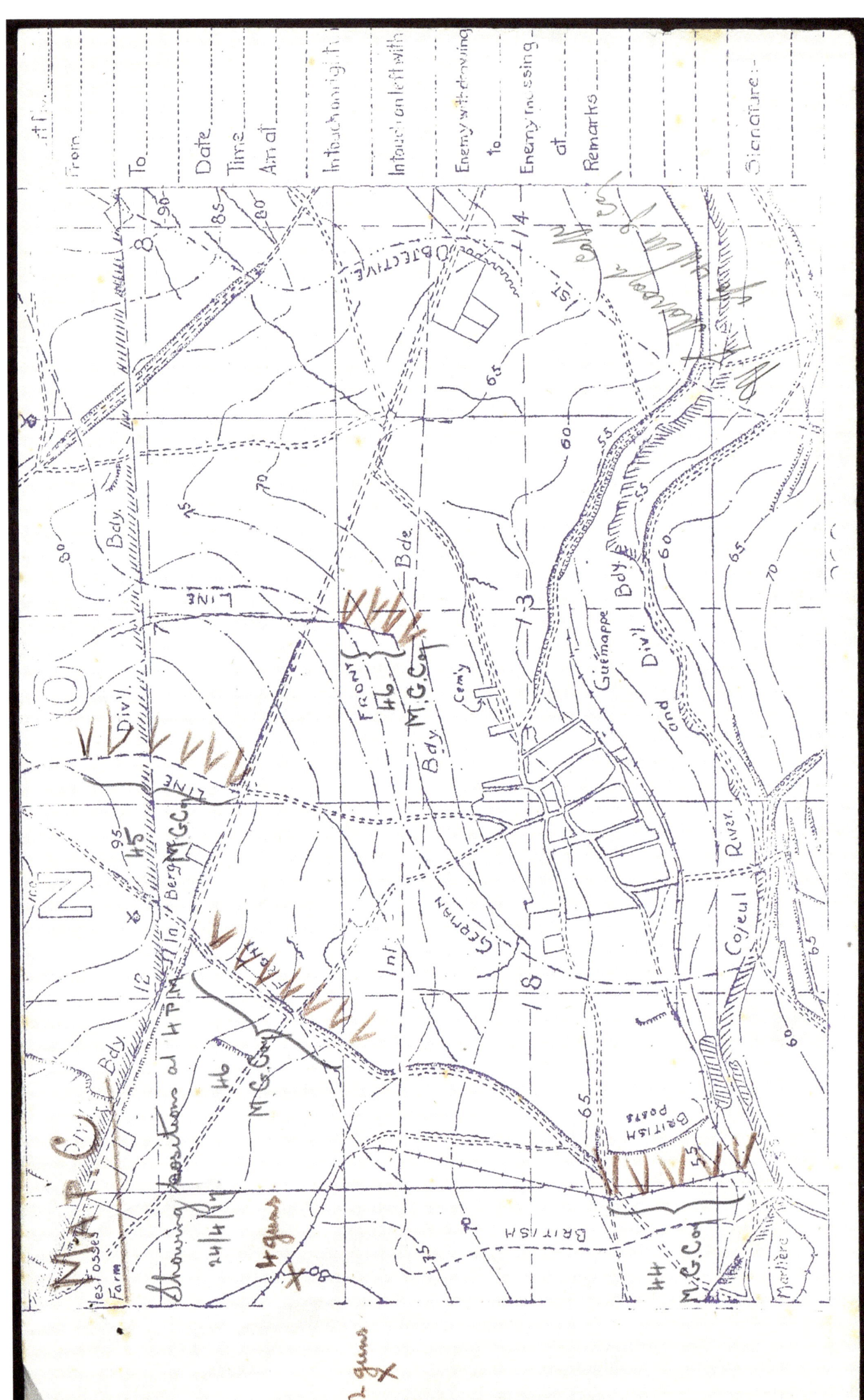

SENT AT 10.15.p.m.

To O.C. E.U.

Message re Stokes mortars received. Own Trench Mortar Officer is reporting to you now.

From L.J.

Vol 16

CONFIDENTIAL

WAR DIARY
of
46th M.G. Company
from 1st May 1917 to 31st May 1917

Vol.

WAR DIARY
or
INTELLIGENCE SUMMARY.

Army Form C. 2118.

Place	Date	Hour	Summary of Events and Information	Remarks and references to Appendices
DUISANS	MAY 1st/6th		In billets at DUISANS. Carried out training programmes as submitted	
"	7th		Left DUISANS for FOSSEUX.	
FOSSEUX	8th/11th		In billets at FOSSEUX, Carried out training programmes as submitted	
"	12th		Brigade Tactical Scheme.	
"	13th		Church Parade	
"	14th		Morning, Carried out usual training. Afternoon Brigade Exercise	
"	15		Training as per programme	

Army Form C. 2118.

WAR DIARY
or
INTELLIGENCE SUMMARY.
(Erase heading not required.)

Instructions regarding War Diaries and Intelligence Summaries are contained in F. S. Regs., Part II. and the Staff Manual respectively. Title pages will be prepared in manuscript.

Place	Date	Hour	Summary of Events and Information	Remarks and references to Appendices
FOSSEUX	MAY 16		Brigade Exercise.	
"	17		One section relieves 151st Infy Brigade at SAULTY engaged in anti-aircraft work.	
"	18/19		Remainder of company carried out usual training	
"	20		Training as per programme	
"			Section at SAULTY relieved by 3rd Divn and joined company at FOSSEUX.	
"	21		Company moved from FOSSEUX to billets in BEAUDRICOURT.	
BEAUDRI-COURT.	22		" " " BEAUDRICOURT to billets in BONNIERES	
BONNIERES	23		" " " BONNIERES to billets in HARAVESNES	

Army Form C. 2118.

WAR DIARY
or
INTELLIGENCE SUMMARY.
(Erase heading not required.)

Place	Date	Hour	Summary of Events and Information	Remarks and references to Appendices
HARAVESNES	MAY 24/31		On billets at HARAVESNES. Carried out training programme as submitted. Company was visited by General Hull M.G.T.C. and transport was inspected by him.	

[Signature]
for O.C.

No. 48 MACHINE GUN COMPANY
DATE 16/17

Vol 17

WAR DIARY

OF

46th Machine Gun Company

FROM 1-6-17
To 30-6-17

VOL :-

Army Form C. 2118.

WAR DIARY
or
INTELLIGENCE SUMMARY.

(Erase heading not required.)

Instructions regarding War Diaries and Intelligence Summaries are contained in F. S. Regs., Part II. and the Staff Manual respectively. Title pages will be prepared in manuscript.

Place	Date	Hour	Summary of Events and Information	Remarks and references to Appendices
A.Q.			Herewith War Diary for June 1917, please.	

No 46 MACHINE GUN COMPANY
DATE 30/6/17

Army Form C. 2118.

WAR DIARY
or
INTELLIGENCE SUMMARY.
(Erase heading not required.)

Instructions regarding War Diaries and Intelligence Summaries are contained in F.S. Regs., Part II. and the Staff Manual respectively. Title pages will be prepared in manuscript.

Place	Date	Hour	Summary of Events and Information	Remarks and references to Appendices
HARAVESNES	JUNE 1		In billets at HARAVESNES. Scheme.	
"	2		Training.	
"	3		Church Parades.	
"	4		Brigade Scheme.	
"	5/6		Carried out Training Programmes.	
"	7/8		Brigade Scheme	
"	9		Carried out Training Programme.	
"	10		Church Parades.	
"	11/12		Carried out Training Programmes	
"	14		Inspection of Coy by Divisional G.O.C. Carried out Field Firing as per Brigade	

A7090. Wt. W18839/M1292. 750,000. 1/17. D, D & L., Ltd. Forms/C2118/14.

Army Form C. 2118.

WAR DIARY
or
INTELLIGENCE SUMMARY.

(Erase heading not required.)

Place	Date	Hour	Summary of Events and Information	Remarks and references to Appendices
HARAVESNES	JUNE 15		Carried out Training Programme	
	16		Company left HARAVESNES at 9.30 P.M and marched to FREVENT and entrained there. Left FREVENT at about 3 A.M on the morning of the 17th and travelled to HOPOUTRE where company detrained and marched to a camp at BRANDHOEK-VLAMERTINGHE and were billeted in tents there.	
	18th		In camp at BRANDHOEK.	
	19.		Company left BRANDHOEK at about 9.30 P.M and marched to the SCHOOL HOUSE, YPRES, taking over their Headquarters from the 23rd M.G Coy	
	20th		Relieved 166th M.G Coy in the line with 10 guns, in front and support lines	

Army Form C. 2118.

WAR DIARY
or
INTELLIGENCE SUMMARY.
(Erase heading not required.)

Instructions regarding War Diaries and Intelligence Summaries are contained in F. S. Regs., Part II. and the Staff Manual respectively. Title pages will be prepared in manuscript.

Place	Date	Hour	Summary of Events and Information	Remarks and references to Appendices
	JUNE 21		In the line. On 23rd inst. Lieut A.K. Pray & H.O.R.'s were gassed by a shell which struck the Company Headquarters	
	24			
	24		One gun in the line blown up & 2 O.R's killed	
	25/26		Into Company relief. One gun blown up on 27th	
	29		Company relieved in the line by 44th M.G. Coy and returned to camp at BRANDHOEK - VLAMERTINGHE.	
	30		In camp.	

M.F. Marragh Capt
O/c 46 M.G.C.

Nov 18

Confidential

War Diary

HQ Machine Gun Corps

n/u 1917

H.Q.

46th I.B.

Herewith War Diary for July 1917, please.

F.W.D. Risher Lieut
O.C.

Army Form C. 2118.

WAR DIARY

INTELLIGENCE SUMMARY.

(Erase heading not required.)

Instructions regarding War Diaries and Intelligence Summaries are contained in F. S. Regs., Part II. and the Staff Manual respectively. Title pages will be prepared in manuscript.

Place	Date	Hour	Summary of Events and Information	Remarks and references to Appendices
BRANDHOEK.	July 1		Company left camp at BRANDHOEK and marched to WATOU TRAINING AREA.	
WATOU	2/7		In billets at WATOU. Carried out training programmes as submitted	
-"-	8		Left WATOU AREA and marched to BROXEELE AREA.	
-"-	"		Billeted at BUYSSCHEURE.	
BUYSSCHEURE	9/12		Carried out training programmes as submitted	
"	13/14		Brigade Tactical Schemes practising the attack.	
"	15/16		Carried out training programmes as submitted.	
"	17		2 sections of Company left BUYSSCHEURE and moved to WINNEZEELE AREA. Remainder of Company carried out training at BUYSSCHEURE	

Army Form C. 2118.

WAR DIARY
or
INTELLIGENCE SUMMARY.
(Erase heading not required.)

Instructions regarding War Diaries and Intelligence Summaries are contained in F. S. Regs., Part II. and the Staff Manual respectively. Title pages will be prepared in manuscript.

Place	Date	Hour	Summary of Events and Information	Remarks and references to Appendices
BUYSSCHEURE	July 18		2 Sections continued march to TORONTO AREA.	
	19		Above 2 Sections left TORONTO CAMP and moved into the line, relieving 6 guns of 45th M.G.Coy (night of 19th/20th)	
	20		2 Sections in the line	
	21		2 Sections in the line. Remainder of company left BROXEELE AREA and marched to WINNEZEELE AREA.	
	22		March continued to WATOU AREA. (2 Guns blown up in the line)	
	23		" " TORONTO AREA	
	24/25		Sections in the line provided working parties for carrying S.A.A., material for shelters, etc and were much hindered by hostile gas shells.	
	26		2 Sections at TORONTO CAMP moved to Advance camp at H.16.a.	
	29/30		Night of 29/30th. Company moved into battle positions in the line	

A5834 Wt. W4973/M687 750,000 8/16 D.D.&L. Ltd. Forms/C.2118/13

Narrative of Operations commencing on 31/7/17.

At ZERO (3.50 A.M) on 31/7/17, my company was disposed as follows:—

2 guns attached to the 10th A.S.I. } in CAMBRIDGE TRENCH.
2 "   "   "   " " 7/8th K.O.S.B. "
4 "   "   in reserve in ST. JAMES TRENCH.
8 "   "   of 46th M.G. Coy } Engaged on Barrage fire at I.4.d.9.2.
8 "   "   " 47th " "   } and I.4.d.9.8 respectively.

At 3.50 A.M. on the 31/7/17 all guns opened fire on their first barrage lines on which they fired for 18 mins. They then lifted to their second barrage lines at ZERO + 19 mins. and fired thereon until ZERO + 1 hr 5 mins. They then lifted on to their third lines and fired from ZERO + 1 hr. 6 mins until ZERO + 1 hr. 23 mins.

In every case the depression stops were set for the range to the targets to avoid any possibility of the guns firing too low.

Army Form C. 2118.

WAR DIARY
INTELLIGENCE SUMMARY.
(Erase heading not required.)

Place	Date	Hour	Summary of Events and Information	Remarks and references to Appendices
			The barrage worked very well indeed and from subsequent prisoners' statements was very effective and caused many casualties to their relieving troops. The barrage guns of my company were under the command of Lieut. W.H. Reavis who was assisted by 2/Lt. T.W. Arch. At ZERO + 1 hr 25 mins, Lieut A.R. Stoker went forward to reconnoitre and choose the second barrage position which was at C.30.b. to 35.a.2. This was done in a very efficient manner despite heavy shell fire. The guns then moved up to their new position, arriving there at ZERO + 2 hrs 10 mins. They were very quickly brought into action and fired a belt of rapid fire on their previously prepared S.O.S. lines which was a protective Barrage for the Black line. At ZERO + 6 hrs. 8 mins They again opened fire on their pre-arranged Barrage lines to cover the advance of the 45th Infy Brigade on to the Green line. They lifted at ZERO + 6 hrs 32 mins on to their second Barrage line	

WAR DIARY

INTELLIGENCE SUMMARY.

(Erase heading not required.)

Army Form C. 2118.

Place	Date	Hour	Summary of Events and Information	Remarks and references to Appendices
			for this position, and fired until ZERO + 6 hrs 46 mins. Lieut A R Stoker then again went forward to SQUARE FARM to reconnoitre, and found the advance to the Green line was progressing forward. A position was then taken up about 30 yds in front of SQUARE FARM from which a protective Barrage for the Green line could be put down in the event of an "S.O.S." being put up, and which also gave a direct command of the ridge in front of HILL 35, in the event of an enemy counter attack being successful. At about ZERO + 7 hrs. 30 mins. we heard that our infantry had established themselves on HILL 35, but later, that they had retired a short distance. At about this time, an enemy aeroplane flew over our line at a low altitude for about 10 minutes and signalled to their artillery by means of coloured lights. SQUARE FARM was made a strong point, our reserve line	

Army Form C. 2118.

WAR DIARY
INTELLIGENCE SUMMARY.
(Erase heading not required.)

Instructions regarding War Diaries and Intelligence Summaries are contained in F. S. Regs., Part II. and the Staff Manual respectively. Title pages will be prepared in manuscript.

Place	Date	Hour	Summary of Events and Information	Remarks and references to Appendices
			At zero + 8 hrs 15 mins. two of the guns in reserve with the 124th A.S.J. moved out to SQUARE FARM, so that 10 guns of my company were then disposed in the vicinity of this strong point. At about 5 P.M. on ZERO day the enemy were reported to be massing at HILL 35. Gun parties were immediately disposed by one on the ridge close to HILL 35, but were immediately dispersed by our fire. At 6.30 P.M., under the orders of the Brigadier, the remaining two reserve guns under Lieut A D Vaughan, moved out into positions for defence of the Pilem line. At this hour the guns were disposed as follows:— 2 guns under Lt A D Vaughan about C.30.d.1.3. 10 " " Lieuts: A R Stoker, R S Luckett, J W Arch, disposed in defensive and barrage positions in the vicinity of SQUARE FARM. 2 guns (attd 1/8 K.O.S.B.) under Lt E F Qualtrough in position in FREZENBERG REDOUBT about D.25.c 30.70. 1 gun (atta 10/11 H.L.I.) under 2/Lt F R Kendrick at about D.25.d 4.8.	

WAR DIARY

INTELLIGENCE SUMMARY

Army Form C. 2118.

Instructions regarding War Diaries and Intelligence Summaries are contained in F. S. Regs., Part II. and the Staff Manual respectively. Title pages will be prepared in manuscript.

(Erase heading not required.)

Place	Date	Hour	Summary of Events and Information	Remarks and references to Appendices
			2/Lt. Hendricks right team under Sergt. Scott went to the assistance of the 4/5th duty Rifles in the attack on the Green line. During the attack, Sergt. Scott and one of the gunners were wounded, and the remaining private, Pirate Clark, took charge. The position appears to have been taken up about 100 yards in front of BECK HOUSE. On 7.4.1 day Lieut. Vaughan's sub-section received orders from me to take up a position at GREY RUIN and the guns were laid on "S.O.S." Barrage lines (D.20.a.4.3.) N°207/41 to D/14.6.4.0. During the day, small parties of the enemy were engaged and dispersed by the guns at FREZENBERG REDOUBT. At about 3 P.M. news was received at SQUARE FARM by wireless that the enemy was counter-attacking on our right, and later the guns under Lieut. Stocker opened fire on their Barrage lines. The shelling in the vicinity of SQUARE FARM. increased in intensity and at about 6 P.M. one gun team of 6 men was entirely wiped out by a shell which	

Army Form C. 2118.

WAR DIARY

INTELLIGENCE SUMMARY.

(Erase heading not required.)

struck the parados of the trench. During this counter attack, BECK HOUSE and BORRY FARM appear to have been occupied by the enemy and it would appear that the gun team under 2/Lt Leleu fell into the hands of the enemy.

On 2+2 day at 4 A.M. No 1 Section gun (Lieut Quilliamy and 2/Lt. Kendrick) were relieved by guns of 45th M.G. Coy. These teams proceeded to the ECOLE where they were joined by the teams of No 4 Section (Lieut Vaughan) "D" Batten. Barrage guns, (Lieuts Stoker, 2/Lieuts Brickett and Arch) remaining in the line under the order of the 115th Inf. Bgde.

During the afternoon the enemy again counter-attacked on the right, but was not seen from SQUARE FARM., although he was reported as being in occupation of BORRY FARM and BECK HOUSE. While very light and Golden Rain rockets were sent up at from about that neighbourhood

WAR DIARY
or
INTELLIGENCE SUMMARY

(Erase heading not required.)

Army Form C. 2118.

Place	Date	Hour	Summary of Events and Information	Remarks and references to Appendices
			On 2 + 3 day there were numerous alarms of counter attack which did not appear to develop. Hostile shelling continues severe and the weather conditions were extremely bad. On the night of 2 + 3/4 days the my 8 barrage guns were relieved by guns of 49th M.G. Coy. and relief was completed by 11 P.M. when the company proceeded to BIVOUAC CAMP at H.16.a. The weather throughout the entire operation was extremely unfavourable, but in spite of this great obstacle the efficiency of the guns was in no way otherwise impaired and the ammunition supply was kept up. I cannot speak too highly of the splendid spirit shown by all ranks throughout this trying period. The company suffered in all 47 Casualties the proportion of killed and missing being rather high, 11 in each case. Officer casualties were extremely light, one only being wounded.

(Signed) A. Hamilton. Lt.
O.C. 46 Machine Gun Coy

H.Q.

46th I.B.

Herewith War Diary for
August 1917, please.

F.W.D Rosher Lt
for O.C.

[Stamp: No. 46 MACHINE GUN COMPANY, DATE 5/9/17]

WAR DIARY

From 1st August 1917
To 31st August 1917

Army Form C. 2118.

WAR DIARY

INTELLIGENCE SUMMARY.

(Erase heading not required.)

Instructions regarding War Diaries and Intelligence Summaries are contained in F. S. Regs., Part II. and the Staff Manual respectively. Title pages will be prepared in manuscript.

Place	Date	Hour	Summary of Events and Information	Remarks and references to Appendices
	Aug 1st to 3rd		In the line	
	4th		Company relieved and marched to WINNEZEELE AREA and were billeted at KIEKENHUT	
	5th to 8th		In billets at KIEKENHUT carried out training programmes as submitted	
	9th		Inspection by Brig. Commander.	
	10th to 15th		Carried out training programmes as submitted.	
	15th		C.Q.M.S. Holden J.T. left the Company and proceeded to join 106th M.G.Coy as C.S.M. The N.C.O. has been with the Company since it came out from England and as he has always performed his duties in the most satisfactory manner his loss was much regretted.	
	16th		The Company left KIEKENHUT and proceeded by march route to ABEELE and there entrained to KRUISTRAAT. After detrainment the Company proceeded to a Camp at H.16.a.5.9.	

Army Form C. 2118.

WAR DIARY
or
INTELLIGENCE SUMMARY.
(Erase heading not required.)

Place	Date	Hour	Summary of Events and Information	Remarks and references to Appendices
			Narrative of Operations from 17/8/17 to 30/31/8/17	

On the night of 17/18th inst, 46th M.G. Coy relieved 49th M.G. Coy (16th Division) in the YPRES Salient.

8 guns under the command of Lt. A.R. Stoker and 2/Lt. R. S. Brackett were at SQUARE FARM.

4 guns under the command of 2/Lt. T. W. Arch and 2/Lt. A. G. Hartley were at FREZENBERG CROSS ROADS.

The relief was successfully carried out under quiet conditions.

4 guns at SQUARE FARM were on "S.O.S." lines covering from North of MARTHA HOUSE to South of DELVA FARM the remaining 4 were on "S.O.S." lines from North of BREMEN REDOUBT to ROULERS RAILWAY.

The 4 guns at FREZENBERG covered the gap.

On the 18th, 19th & 20th continuous work was carried on in improving the positions which, owing to the & weather conditions were in very poor condition. Hostile shelling was at times very heavy, but owing

WAR DIARY
INTELLIGENCE SUMMARY

Army Form C. 2118.

Place	Date	Hour	Summary of Events and Information	Remarks and references to Appendices

to the fortification afforded by SQUARE FARM and cement emplacement at FREZENBERG REDOUBT. Our casualties were not heavy. On the night of the 19/20th, we cooperated with infantry with a twelve Stokes bombardment. Unfortunately Sergt. Stead, No.2 Section, who had been with the Company since its formation, was wounded by a shell splinter and was obliged to return to the Dressing Station and was relieved by the 44th & 145th Lt. Bgds. T.M.G. boys and were withdrawn to Ramery. On the night of the 20/21st, all guns were removed from the position just in rear of GREY.RUIN which had been permanently recommended by Lt. I/c N.D.Rocher, Lt. A.R. Stocker was myself. The 16 guns were divided into 2 Batteries. 1 & 3 Section on the right forming "C" Battery, 2 & 4 Sections on the left forming "D" Battery, 2/Lt A.R. Stocker was in charge of "D" Battery and 2/Lt. J. is Arnot in charge of "C" Battery. In spite of heavy shelling and bad conditions, the men worked splendidly at making their new positions and existing shelter.

WAR DIARY

INTELLIGENCE SUMMARY

On the 21st work was still continued on the Barrage Route.
At the 4.45 A.M. on the 22nd the 14th and 154th Infy Brigades attacked the line KANGA'S CROSS ROADS south to the RAILWAY.
The guns of the company cooperated and fired from "KERO" until which they lifted to their second Barrage line on KERO + 26 mins, they fired from "KERO + 26 mins until "KERO + 46 mins. We rate of fire being in the first case 1 bullet in 4 mins and in the second case 1 bullet in 2 mins.
Enemy shelling was not heavy during the attack but about 6 A.M a heavy hostile barrage was put down on GREY RUIN RIDGE.
The company had several casualties amt to 3 guns knocked out.
On the evening of the 22nd. Lieut A.D. Taylor and 2/Lt F.R. Kenwick reliered the Officers at the Barrage gun and as many men as possible were relieved and withdrawn from the position. Minimal casualties. The hostile artillery still continues to be very heavy and several casualties occurred.

WAR DIARY

INTELLIGENCE SUMMARY

(Erase heading not required.)

Army Form C. 2118.

Instructions regarding War Diaries and Intelligence Summaries are contained in F. S. Regs., Part II. and the Staff Manual respectively. Title pages will be prepared in manuscript.

Place	Date	Hour	Summary of Events and Information	Remarks and references to Appendices
			On the 23rd the Company were relieved by 225th M.G. Coy and returned to TORONTO CAMP, Durey. The day, two more guns were destroyed by shell fire and further casualties occurred. Refitting out, general cleaning up was carried out on the 24th. inst. On the 25th, Sgt A. Strawhorn, L/Cpl R. Stanfields & A. Dyke and J. Doherty were awarded the Military Medal, for gallantry in the field. On the 26th, refitting and resting. 2/Lt O. R. Stratton and 2/Lt A. reconnoitred positions about 500 x in rear of GREY RUIN for 16 guns to support the 14th Brigade attack on the 28th. Lieut A. R. Starker was sent on the 27th inst. 2/Lt P.D. Osborne and 14 men as an advance party to get the positions reconnoitred on the 26th. known. In the evening 14 guns under the command of 2/Lt S. J. R. Henderson, 2/Lt A. J. Hartley, 2/Lt A. R. Starker, 2/Lt P.D. Osborne & Lieut A.D. Vaughan occupied the position already mentioned. In spite of	

WAR DIARY

INTELLIGENCE SUMMARY

(Erase heading not required.)

Army Form C. 2118.

Instructions regarding War Diaries and Intelligence Summaries are contained in F. S. Regs., Part II. and the Staff Manual respectively. Title pages will be prepared in manuscript.

Place	Date	Hour	Summary of Events and Information	Remarks and references to Appendices
			pouring rain and heavy shelling the men worked splendidly in preparing this position. At about 10.30 P.M. orders were received by me at lay A.Qrs., MILLCOTS that owing to the weather the proposed attack for the 28th was cancelled and my Company was to withdraw after some difficulty little in the ECOLE was found for the men who arrived there very wet, but magnificently cheerful. About 2.A.M. on the 28th the gun material was stored in shelters near the gun positions and a guard left to take care of it. It was presumed on the night of the 28th. On the 28th inst. the company moved back to TORONTO CAMP. On the 29th the guns were re-alloted etc and a general reorganization took place. On the evening we relieved the forward guns on the whole Divisional front from 44th & 115th M.G.Coy. 11 guns in all going into the line, the 5 in reserve being at the ECOLE under Sergt. McDermott. M.M. 2/Lt. F.R. Randwick has charge of 3 guns in SQUARE FARM and 2 in POMMERN CASTLE	

Army Form C. 2118.

WAR DIARY
or
INTELLIGENCE SUMMARY.
(Erase heading not required.)

Place	Date	Hour	Summary of Events and Information	Remarks and references to Appendices
			On the 31st inst. the company remained in camp at H.16.c & 9. Inst cleaning out guns and materials etc	

A Hamilton
OC

Army Form C. 2118.

WAR DIARY
INTELLIGENCE SUMMARY.
(Erase heading not required.)

Place	Date	Hour	Summary of Events and Information	Remarks and references to Appendices
			2/Lt A.G. Hartley had charge of 2 guns, both just south of POMMERN CASTLE 2/Lt Turner had two guns in SQUARE FARM. 2/Lt Peile had two guns in FREKENBERG REDOUBT. 2/Lt R.S. Lovelett had two guns in the "HUTS" about 100 S.E. of FREKENBERG CROSS ROADS. The relief was carried out under fairly quiet conditions. During the night of the 30th we were relieved by 125th M.G. Coy. The guides and cars were excellent although they had never been over the ground once before. Unfortunately the guides to #2 and #4 Guns got lost and his relief was not complete until 4 A.M. 31/8/17. All teams withdrew to camp at H.16.w.5.9. During the second phase the conduct of the Officers and men was in every way splendid and the Company was warmly congratulated by Brigadier General Slade, G.O.C. 46th Infy. Bgde. but this good work was made very trying conditions. The casualties for this phase were :—	Killed 6 Wounded 10 (Lieutenant Lillie) Missing 1

Army Form W.3091.

Cover for Documents.

Nature of Enclosures.

Vol 20

WAR DAIRY
of
46th Machine Gun Company.
From 1st September 1917.
To 30th September 1917.

Notes, or Letters written.

Army Form C. 2113.

WAR DIARY
INTELLIGENCE SUMMARY.
(Erase heading not required.)

Place	Date	Hour	Summary of Events and Information	Remarks and references to Appendices
Sept	1		In camp at H.16.a.5.9. Left camp at 4 A.M. and proceeded by bus route to ZERMEZEELE AREA. and stayed there until evening. Left at 7.30 P.M. and proceeded by march route to CASSEL STATION. Entrained at about 10.30 P.M. and travelled to ARRAS, arriving there at 6.30 A.M. 2/9/17, when the Company detrained and marched to DUISANS.	
Sept	2/5		In billets at DUISANS. Spent the time in generally cleaning up (guns, material & men) also carried out training as per programme.	
Sept	6		Left DUISANS at 5 PM and marched via ARRAS to DINGWALL CAMP G.18.c.h.9. and took over from 45th M.G. Coy. Company now then in Divisional Reserve under the administration of the 4th Division.	
Sept	7		Took over 12 guns in Right Sector of the 15th Divisional front relieving 12th M.G. Coy. by 9 A.m were at H.35.b.5.6.	

WAR DIARY or INTELLIGENCE SUMMARY

Army Form C. 2118.

Place	Date	Hour	Summary of Events and Information	Remarks and references to Appendices
	Sept 6th		In the line. Carried out indirect fire on targets as arranged. Also carried out firing at & from Anti-aircraft positions at hostile aircraft which frequently came over our own lines.	
	23rd		(15th Sept) Inter-Company relief. No 4 Section relieved by No 3.)	
	23rd		Company was relieved in the line by 45th M.G. Coy and returned to billets at DINGWALL CAMP.	
	28th		1 Officer & 16 O.R's of No 3 Section proceeded to LIGNY-ST-FLOCHEL and took over 2 Anti-Aircraft positions there. The teams on Anti-Aircraft duties were relieved by two fresh teams.	
	29th / 30th		In billets at DINGWALL CAMP. The time was occupied in training, cleaning up, etc. and preparing for the line.	

O. Maxwell Capt.
O.C.
46th MACHINE GUN COMPANY
Date 30.9.17

H.Q.

46th J.D.

46th MACHINE GUN COMPANY.
No.
Date 7/11/17

Herewith War Diary for Oct 1917.
please.

W.D. Roth
for O.C

Confidential

Oct 21

War Diary
of
46th Machine Gun Company
for
October 1917

Vol. XX

WAR DIARY
INTELLIGENCE SUMMARY
(Erase heading not required.)

Army Form C. 2118.

Place	Date	Hour	Summary of Events and Information	Remarks and references to Appendices
	Oct 1st		Took over 12 guns in the line from 44th M.G.Coy, in the left sector of the 15th Divisional Front.	
	Oct 1st to 13th		In the line. Carried out indirect firing on enemy trenches and tracks in cooperation with the artillery as arranged. Firing was also carried out from anti-aircraft positions at hostile aircraft. The strength of the Company on the 15th inst was 10 Officers & 210 Other Ranks. On the 14th inst the guns fired in cooperation with the raid made by 12th Divn.	
	14th		On the 14th inst the Company were relieved in the line by 45th M.G.Coy, and returned to ARRAS, being billeted in RUE DE TURENNE.	
	14th to 24th		In billets in ARRAS. The time was spent in cleaning up (men and material) training, (as per programme submitted) and preparing guns and men for the line.	

Army Form C. 2118.

WAR DIARY
or
INTELLIGENCE SUMMARY
(Erase heading not required.)

Place	Date	Hour	Summary of Events and Information	Remarks and references to Appendices
	Oct 25th		The company (less 1 Section) left ARRAS and proceeded to the line taking over 12 guns in the Right Sector of the 15th Divisional Front from 44th M.G.Coy (bay. A.Gn. at H.36.t 50.5) The remaining section was in Brigade Coy Reserve and was billeted at WILDERNESS CAMP (H.31.a)	
	25th to 31st		In the line. Indirect firing was carried out on targets as arranged and firing was also done at hostile aircraft.	

46th MACHINE GUN COMPANY.
No............
Date 2/11/17

A Accumulator Corpl.
6/2

CONFIDENTIAL

WM 22

WAR DIARY
OF
46th M.G. COMPANY
FOR
NOVEMBER 1917

Army Form C. 2118.

WAR DIARY
or
INTELLIGENCE SUMMARY.
(Erase heading not required.)

Instructions regarding War Diaries and Intelligence Summaries are contained in F.S. Regs., Part II. and the Staff Manual respectively. Title pages will be prepared in manuscript.

Place	Date	Hour	Summary of Events and Information	Remarks and references to Appendices
	Nov. 1st to 9th		In the line in Right Sector of the 15th Divisional Front, Company Headquarters at H.36.b.5.5. Carried out Indirect firing on the enemy's trenches, and tracks as arranged in cooperation with the Artillery, and fire was also carried out from Anti-Aircraft positions at hostile aircraft.	
	10th		Relieved by 145th M.G. Coy., and proceeded to Billets in ARRAS, RUE de TURENNE.	
	11th to 14th		In billets in ARRAS. The time was spent in cleaning up (men, and material) training (as per programme submitted), and preparing guns, and men for the line.	
	18th		Relieved 144th M.G. Coy in the left Sector of the 15th Divisional Front. 15 guns were in the line, and 1 gun in reserve at Company Headquarters H.23.c.4.9.	
	28th & 29th		The 15th Division took over the 61st Divisional front, the ROEUX Sector thus becoming the Right Sector of the Divisional front. On the 28th Nos 1, and 13 M.G. positions of 184 M.G. Coy were taken over by the Company. During the early days of this period in the line we adopted an especially agreed policy of cooperation with the operations before CAMBRAI.	
	30th		Still in the line all 16 guns being in positions.	

J.W. R ... for O.C.

Vol 23

War Diary
of
46th Machine Gun Coy
for
December 1917.

Army Form C. 2118.

WAR DIARY
INTELLIGENCE SUMMARY.
(Erase heading not required.)

Instructions regarding War Diaries and Intelligence Summaries are contained in F. S. Regs., Part II. and the Staff Manual respectively. Title pages will be prepared in manuscript.

Place	Date	Hour	Summary of Events and Information	Remarks and references to Appendices
	1917 DEC.1 to DEC.7		The Company were in the line in the Right Sector of the Divisional Front, all 16 guns being in positions. Indirect fire was carried out on various targets, (enemy's tracks, trenches, etc) in cooperation with the Artillery programme.	
	DEC.8		The Company were relieved in the line by 45th M.G. Coy and then returned to billets in ARRAS.	
	DEC.10		On the night of the 10/11th, the company were ordered to the bombs and Intermediate line in anticipation of a hostile attack which was expected to take place the next morning. 14 positions were occupied and 2 guns and team were left in reserve at ARRAS.	
	DEC.11		The teams in the bombs line were relieved by 44th M.G. Coy and they then proceeded to the Left Sector of the Divisional front, accompanied by the two teams which were in ARRAS, and took over the positions occupied by 44th M.G. Coy. 16 guns being then in positions	

CONTINUED

Army Form C. 2118.

WAR DIARY
or
INTELLIGENCE SUMMARY.
(Erase heading not required.)

46th MACHINE GUN COMPANY.
No. ....
Date 31.12.17

Place	Date	Hour	Summary of Events and Information	Remarks and references to Appendices
	1917			
	DEC 16 to DEC 31		In the line. Indirect fire was carried out on various targets (enemy's tracks, trenches, etc) in co-operation with the artillery programme. Firing was also carried out at hostile aircraft.	
			On the 29th inst. No. 7959 SGT. BENNETT. W. left the company on being promoted Colour Sergeant and being appointed C.Q.M.S. for duty with No. 11. M.G. Coy. SGT. BENNETT W had served with this company continuously from the time of its formation in England in Dec. 1915 at to the time of his departure. During this period he has been a Section Sergt, Acting C.S.M. for a period of about 6 months, and Acting C.Q.M.S for a few weeks. He has always proven himself to be most efficient and trustworthy and has at all times discharged his duties in a very conscientious manner. His loss is greatly regretted by the company as it will be difficult to replace such a capable N.C.O.	A Hawelli Capt Comdg

CASUALTIES DURING THE MONTH 1 O.R. WOUNDED
STRENGTH OF THE COMPANY { 15th INST. 10 OFF. 214 O.R.
                          { 31st "   10 OFF. 210 O.R.

CONFIDENTIAL

Vol 24

WAR DIARY

OF

46th M.G. COMPANY

FOR

JANUARY 1918.

(50)

Confidential.

CONFIDENTIAL

AQ

46th I D.

Enclosed please find War Diary for
January 1918.

H Vaughan Lieut
for OC

Army Form C. 2118.

WAR DIARY
or
INTELLIGENCE SUMMARY.
(Erase heading not required.)

Instructions regarding War Diaries and Intelligence Summaries are contained in F. S. Regs., Part II. and the Staff Manual respectively. Title pages will be prepared in manuscript.

46th MACHINE GUN COMPANY. Date 2.2.45

Place	Date	Hour	Summary of Events and Information	Remarks and references to Appendices
	1916 Jan 1		The Company were relieved in the Left Sector of the Divisional Front by the 3rd Guards Brigade Machine Gun Company and marched to billets in ARRAS.	
	Jan 2		The Company left ARRAS at 2 P.M. and proceeded by march route to BERNEVILLE and went into billets.	
	Jan 3 to Jan 31		In billets at BERNEVILLE. Carried out training on the programme submitted, including several tactical schemes which were carried out in conjunction with the Battalions of the Brigade.	

CASUALTIES DURING MONTH :- NIL.
COMPANY'S STRENGTH 15th inst. 10 Officers. 211 O.R's
" " 31st " 10 " 194 "

[signature]

WAR DIARY
or
INTELLIGENCE SUMMARY.
(Erase heading not required.)

Army Form C. 2118.

Place	Date	Hour	Summary of Events and Information	Remarks and references to Appendices
BERNEVILLE	FEB 15th		In billets at BERNEVILLE. Carried out training as per programmes submitted.	
ARRAS	6th		The company left BERNEVILLE and proceeded by march route to ARRAS and were billeted.	
ARRAS	6/8th		In billets at ARRAS. The time was spent in cleaning and preparing guns for the line	
	8th		3 Sections and Company Headquarters proceeded to the line and take over 10 guns from the 45th Machine Gun Company in the left sector of the 15th Divl. Front. Company Hd Qrs at H.35.b.5.5.	
	8th/28th		In the line. Section relief took place on 13th, 18th, 23rd & 28th inst. On the 22nd inst. work was commenced building dug-outs, shelters and machine gun nests at various gun positions. This work was carried out by the personnel of the gun teams at the various gun positions.	

Vol. 25

War Diary
of
46th M.G. Company

WAR DIARY
or
INTELLIGENCE SUMMARY

On the 23rd inst., 6 guns fired a barrage in cooperation with the successful raid made by the 4th Cameron Highlanders.

COMPANY STRENGTH. 14TH. INST. 10 OFFICERS 192 O.R's
                   "   28TH.   9   "   188 O.R's

CASUALTIES FOR MONTH. NIL

www.ingramcontent.com/pod-product-compliance
Lightning Source LLC
Chambersburg PA
CBHW081408160426
43193CB00013B/2129